Alex Cisneros is a barrister at 39 Essex Chambers, specialising in mental capacity law. He regularly acts for public bodies, the Office of the Public Guardian, the Official Solicitor and families in complex disputes concerning capacity, best interests and financial decision-making. He has appeared in two guidance cases concerning the drafting and management of Lasting Powers of Attorney in England and Wales. He delivers regular training on LPAs and mental capacity law both nationally and internationally.

Alex is also a trustee of POhWER and is actively involved in policy discussion across the mental capacity and social care sectors. Alongside his practice, he has an academic background in mental capacity law and is due to defend his PhD on the subject later this year.

A Practical Guide to Lasting Powers of Attorney

A Practical Guide to Lasting Powers of Attorney

Alex Cisneros
Barrister, Middle Temple

Law Brief Publishing

Published 2026 by Law Brief Publishing, an imprint of Law Brief Publishing Ltd
30 The Parks
Minehead
Somerset
TA24 8BT

www.lawbriefpublishing.com

Paperback: 978-1-918241-18-1

PREFACE

This book was written in 2025 and brings together several years of practice, research and reflection on how people plan for a time when they may no longer be able to make decisions for themselves. It looks at how those plans work in real life, within families, professional settings and the courts. Lasting Powers of Attorney are now a central part of legal practice, but their apparent simplicity hides difficult questions about independence, trust and control. My aim has been to explain the law clearly, without losing sight of the people whose lives these documents affect.

I am grateful to the many people who helped shape this book. I owe particular thanks to colleagues and clients who shared their experiences.

My greatest thanks go to my clerks at 39 Essex Chambers, whose patience and support throughout the writing of this book have been remarkable.

All statutory and case law references in this work are accurate as at 19 January 2026.

Alex Cisneros
January 2026

CONTENTS

CHAPTER ONE

HISTORICAL AND LEGAL CONTEXT

1. Introduction

Lasting Powers of Attorney (LPAs) now form one of the most commonly used legal instruments in private client practice. Their prevalence is particularly striking when compared with their short history: LPAs have existed for less than two decades, yet they underpin the financial, personal and welfare arrangements of millions of people. For practitioners, LPAs are not merely forms to be completed, but documents with profound legal implications. An LPA shapes who may make decisions, how authority is exercised, what safeguards apply and how autonomy is protected when a person's decision-making abilities are impaired.

This introductory chapter situates LPAs within their broader historical and legal context. It outlines the evolution from Enduring Powers of Attorney, explains the policy aims underpinning the Mental Capacity Act 2005 (MCA 2005), and examines the demographic and social pressures that shaped reform. It also introduces the supervisory role of the Office of the Public Guardian (OPG) and explains how LPAs fit within the wider mental capacity framework, including their relationship with best interests decision-making, the Court of Protection, and professional practice.

This background is more than scene-setting: understanding the origins and structure of the current framework is essential for analysing some of the challenges LPAs create in practice. As LPAs continue to develop and new questions emerge, a firm grasp of the statutory context becomes increasingly important.

2. Development from Enduring Powers of Attorney to LPAs

This principle of agency underpins the modern law of powers of attorney. As HHJ Hilder observed in Re *Various Lasting Powers of Attorney* [2019] EWCOP 40 (§7):

> "It was long ago recognised at common law that people need not always do for themselves things that change their legal relations with the world – they may instead authorise someone else to do those things for them."

However, until the mid-1980s this common-law authority had a fundamental limitation: any general power of attorney automatically ceased the moment the donor lost mental capacity. The Enduring Powers of Attorney Act 1985 was the first significant statutory reform to overcome that barrier. It introduced the EPA, allowing individuals in England and Wales to appoint someone to manage their financial affairs *after* they lost capacity. Before this development, those who became unwell or cognitively impaired were left in a precarious position, dependent on the old receivership process and without any private, proactive mechanism for protecting their financial autonomy.

EPAs were therefore widely welcomed. For the first time, a donor could choose trusted individuals to manage their affairs and rely on the instrument to continue operating even after they became unable to make their own decisions. This significantly reduced the need for court intervention and allowed families to plan ahead with greater confidence.

Yet from the start, EPAs showed several weaknesses that later reforms sought to address. The most significant issue was the lack of oversight. An EPA did not need to be registered unless the attorney believed the donor was starting to lose capacity, and until that point the attorney could act with virtually no external scrutiny. In practice, this meant that attorneys could exercise considerable financial power long before anyone else became aware.

This linked closely to a second problem: uncertainty around registration. Attorneys were required to register the EPA when the donor was "becoming or had become mentally incapable,"[1] but the trigger point was vague and easy to manipulate. Some attorneys delayed registration precisely because it would bring their actions under closer supervision, creating opportunities for misuse.

Safeguarding concerns were a consistent theme. As public awareness of elder financial abuse grew, it became increasingly clear that EPAs lacked the protective mechanisms needed to identify or prevent exploitation. There was no certification process, no structured assessment of capacity at the time the EPA was granted, and no obligatory checks to confirm that the donor was acting freely.

EPAs also sat awkwardly alongside the emerging modern understanding of mental capacity. Developed in the 1980s, they predated the decision-specific, functional capacity test that would later be central to the MCA 2005. As a result, the EPA system struggled to balance autonomy, protection and clarity in the way that later frameworks sought to achieve.

Finally, EPAs were confined to financial and property matters. They offered no mechanism for delegating health or welfare decisions, leaving those areas governed by the common law best interests test. This gap became increasingly visible as families sought clearer, more comprehensive ways to plan for declining capacity.

These limitations did not undermine the importance of EPAs as a pioneering reform, but they laid the groundwork for the more robust, more regulated, and more comprehensive system of Lasting Powers of Attorney that would follow under the MCA 2005.

---

1 Section 4(1) of the Enduring Powers of Attorney Act 1985

3. Policy objectives of the MCA 2005

The MCA 2005 marked a fundamental turning point in the law of substitute decision-making. One of its most significant reforms was the replacement of Enduring Powers of Attorney with a new, more sophisticated regime: the Lasting Power of Attorney. For the first time, donors were able to create two distinct instruments, one governing property and financial affairs, and another allowing a chosen attorney to make health and welfare decisions. This move reflected a conceptual shift away from the narrow financial focus of EPAs and towards a much broader view of personal autonomy and future planning.

The MCA 2005 introduced a comprehensive statutory framework that placed LPAs at the heart of modern capacity law. Three ideas shaped the overhaul: the need for a more regulated and robust alternative to EPAs, the desire to embed all aspects of capacity within a single coherent statute, and the creation of institutions capable of supervising and enforcing the new system. The establishment of the Office of the OPG and the reconstituted Court of Protection were central to this design.

Although EPAs could no longer be created after October 2007, those made before that date remain valid and registrable. Practitioners still encounter them, particularly when dealing with long-standing donors whose affairs have not been updated. Nevertheless, LPAs now dominate practice. They have become the default planning tool and, in most cases, offer greater flexibility, protection and clarity than the older EPA model.

LPAs introduced several important innovations. Perhaps the most significant was the requirement for a certificate provider (discussed further in Chapter Four), someone independent who could confirm that the donor had capacity and was not being pressured into granting the LPA. This safeguard addressed the long-standing concerns about undue influence that had plagued the EPA system. LPAs also expanded the scope of decision-making authority by allowing attorneys to act in relation to personal welfare, including, where expressly authorised, life-sustaining treatment decisions (discussed in Chapter Two). The requirement for immediate registration removed the uncertainty of the EPA regime, where attorneys had to decide when the donor was "becoming incapable," often leading to delayed registration and reduced oversight. Under the new system, the LPA is registered at the outset, providing a clear, verifiable record of its validity.

LPAs were intended to be straightforward to create, clear in their structure, user-friendly and adaptable to a variety of family arrangements. The system was designed so that non-lawyers could use it without prohibitive expense, while still retaining sufficient safeguards to protect vulnerable donors. In practice, these ambitions have not always been fully realised. Registration delays, execution errors and complex family situations can create obstacles, and the evolution towards digitalisation reflects an ongoing attempt to make the system more efficient and secure.

Overall, the replacement of EPAs with LPAs, and the broader statutory framework of the MCA 2005, represents a deliberate shift towards enhancing autonomy, strengthening safeguards and providing clarity. For practitioners, understanding this context is essential. LPAs do not simply grant authority: they sit within a nuanced legal and ethical framework that governs how that authority must be exercised, supervised, and, when necessary, challenged.

4. Oversight by the Office of the Public Guardian

The OPG was created by the MCA 2005 as part of the Act's wider project of embedding substitute decision-making within a clear and supervised statutory structure. The MCA sets out the OPG's functions in section 58, placing it at the heart of the LPA and deputyship regime. From the outset, its principal purpose has been to safeguard people who lack capacity by supervising those who make decisions on their behalf. This supervisory role is broad and multi-layered, ranging from the routine administrative work of registering LPAs to the far more interventionist task of investigating misconduct.

For most practitioners, the OPG's most visible function is the registration of LPAs. Every LPA must be registered before it can be used, and the MCA 2005 makes registration a mandatory safeguard rather than an optional step. Because the instrument is scrutinised before it becomes active, the OPG can identify issues such as defective execution, unlawful or unclear instructions, problematic preferences, missing notifications or concerns about undue influence. It can also pick up eligibility issues where, for example, an attorney lacks capacity, is a bankrupt (in the case of financial LPAs), or otherwise does not meet the statutory criteria. The registration process has therefore become one of the most effective protective mechanisms in the entire statutory scheme. A practitioner who understands how the OPG approaches registration (addressed throughout this book), what it queries, what it will accept, and what it will sever, significantly reduces the risk of applications being rejected or delayed.

The MCA 2005 also gives the OPG strong investigatory powers. Under section 58, the OPG has a duty to supervise deputies appointed by the Court of Protection and to investigate complaints or concerns about attorneys acting under LPAs or EPAs. These investigations can arise from a variety of concerns: suspected financial abuse, neglect of a donor's welfare, conflicts of interest, misuse of donor funds or a failure to act in the donor's best interests. The latter is especially significant, as the best interests requirement is grounded in section 4 of the MCA and applies to all substitute decision-makers. There are also cases where the OPG becomes involved because an attorney appears to be acting outside the scope of their authority, whether by exceeding financial powers or making welfare decisions that were not delegated. Investigations of this kind often culminate in an application to the Court of Protection to remove an attorney or to seek directions. The courts take these matters extremely seriously.

Practitioners typically interact with the OPG at several points, including:

- during the LPA registration process;

- when corresponding with the OPG about execution or formality queries;
- when responding to requests for further information or clarification;
- when making safeguarding referrals to the OPG or receiving contact following a referral; and
- when involved in disputes between attorneys, family members or other interested parties, where the OPG may act as a mediator or investigator before any court proceedings are issued.

Being familiar with the OPG's practice notes, application guidance and internal expectations can make a substantial difference to client outcomes. Many delays arise not from legal complexity but from avoidable issues such as unclear drafting, misaligned preferences and instructions, or incomplete notification procedures.

In recent years, the OPG has undertaken a significant modernisation programme to make LPAs more secure, more accessible and better suited to digital processes. Its website now provides a growing body of guidance, including practical documents and regular briefing updates. Practitioners should familiarise themselves with this guidance and keep it under review, as it increasingly shapes how LPAs are processed and scrutinised in practice.

5. The LPA in the wider mental capacity framework

LPAs sit within the wider framework of the MCA 2005, which governs both how attorneys may act and when their authority begins. Central to this framework is the Act's statutory definition of capacity (discussed further in Chapter Five). The MCA establishes a functional, decision-specific test: a person lacks capacity only if, at the material time, they are unable to understand, retain, use or weigh, or communicate information relevant to the decision in question. This approach ensures that capacity is not treated as a blanket status but assessed carefully each time a decision arises. It respects autonomy by recognising that individuals may be able to make some decisions even when they need support with others.

Whenever a donor lacks capacity, the attorney must turn to the statutory best interests framework. The MCA requires attorneys to look far beyond mere welfare or convenience. They must consider the donor's past and present wishes, consult relevant people (including family members and professionals), take into account the donor's beliefs and values, and identify the course of action that is least restrictive of the donor's rights and freedoms.

Alongside these duties sits the Court of Protection, which plays a central role in interpreting, policing and, when necessary, correcting the use of LPAs (discussed in Chapter Eight). The Court may resolve disputes between attorneys or between attorneys and family members; remove an attorney who is acting improperly; declare an LPA invalid if it was improperly executed or granted without capacity; interpret ambiguous or conflicting instructions; and decide whether the donor had capacity at the point the LPA was created. The Court also has exclusive jurisdiction to authorise transactions that fall outside an attorney's authority, such as significant gifts or major financial restructuring. Practitioners need to be alert to situations where court intervention becomes necessary, particularly in complex or contentious matters, for example, decisions about serious medical treatment, high-value financial decisions, disputes between attorneys, allegations of misconduct, or decisions involving intricate business arrangements.

Health and Welfare LPAs frequently intersect with other legal and clinical frameworks (discussed in Chapter Six). They may operate alongside advance decisions to refuse treatment, care plans, NHS decision-making processes and safeguarding investigations. Where there is a conflict between an attorney's authority and an advance decision, the MCA provides a clear hierarchy: a valid and applicable advance decision takes precedence unless the donor has specifically conferred authority on the attorney to make decisions about life-sustaining treatment. Practitioners must therefore be careful to identify and reconcile these instruments before advising on or implementing medical decisions.

In this way, LPAs do not operate in isolation. They are woven through the broader mental capacity landscape, defined and constrained by the MCA's principles, supervised by the Court of Protection, and shaped by the practical realities of modern health and social care. Understanding these relationships is essential for practitioners who wish to navigate the regime effectively and safeguard their clients' interests.

CHAPTER TWO

TYPES OF LPA

1. Introduction

Lasting Powers of Attorney were designed to be deceptively simple. At their core, they allow a person (the donor) to choose trusted individuals (attorneys) to take decisions on their behalf if they lose mental capacity in the future. Yet the statutory framework set out in the MCA 2005, combined with the variation in donors' personal, financial and familial circumstances, means that LPAs operate on far more than a simple administrative level.

This chapter examines the evolution, purpose and operation of the different types of LPAs: Property and Financial Affairs LPAs and Health and Welfare LPAs. Although donors and professionals frequently treat LPAs as standardised forms, the real skill lies in recognising that these instruments can be moulded to suit a donor's personal and financial structure. At their best, LPAs ensure continuity, protect vulnerable individuals from exploitation and reflect their personal values even long after they lose decisional capacity. At their worst, poorly drafted LPAs can give rise to disputes, facilitate financial abuse, or impose burdensome duties on attorneys who lack the skills, temperament or impartiality to perform the role. To navigate these tensions, a detailed understanding of each type of LPA is essential.

2. Property and Financial Affairs LPAs

2.1 Purpose and Scope

A Property and Financial Affairs LPA authorises attorneys to make decisions about the donor's financial life. As explained at paragraph 7.36 of the MCA 2005 Code of Practice:

> *If a donor does not restrict decisions the attorney can make, the attorney will be able to decide on any or all of the person's property and financial affairs. This might include:*
>
> - *buying or selling property*
> - *opening, closing or operating any bank, building society or other account*
> - *giving access to the donor's financial information*
> - *claiming, receiving and using (on the donor's behalf) all benefits, pensions, allowances and rebates (unless the Department for Work and Pensions has already appointed someone and everyone is happy for this to continue)*
> - *receiving any income, inheritance or other entitlement on behalf of the donor*
> - *dealing with the donor's tax affairs*
> - *paying the donor's mortgage, rent and household expenses*
> - *insuring, maintaining and repairing the donor's property*
> - *investing the donor's savings*

- *making limited gifts on the donor's behalf (but see paragraphs 7.40–7.42 below)*
- *paying for private medical care and residential care or nursing home fees*
- *applying for any entitlement to funding for NHS care, social care or adaptations*
- *using the donor's money to buy a vehicle or any equipment or other help they need*
- *repaying interest and capital on any loan taken out by the donor.*

Perhaps uniquely among personal-delegation instruments in English law, the Property and affairs LPA sits at the intersection of private fiduciary responsibility and public statutory oversight. The donor appoints the attorney, but the attorney's legal obligations, including the fiduciary duties, duties of care and duties of loyalty, are grounded in statute, and supervised (to a limited extent) by the Office of the OPG.

As Senior Judge Lush (as he was) noted in *The OPG v C* [2013] EWCOP 2965:

> "22. People who have the capacity to manage their own financial affairs are generally not accountable to anyone and don't need to keep accounts or records of their income and expenditure. They can do whatever they like with their money, and this includes doing nothing at all. They can stash their cash under the mattress, if they wish and, of course, they are entitled to make unwise decisions.
>
> 23. None of these options are open to an attorney acting for an incapacitated donor, partly because of their fiduciary obligations and partly because an attorney is required to act

in the donor's best interests. The MCA 2005, section 1(5), states that, "an act done, or decision made, under this Act for or on behalf of a person who lacks capacity must be done, or made, in his best interests."”

A Property and affairs LPA may be used before the donor loses capacity if the donor consents to this. Many donors choose this option so that their attorneys can help manage complex financial portfolios, assist with daily administration such as paying bills, or act in circumstances where the donor is physically incapacitated but retains mental capacity.

Others prefer to restrict the attorney's powers so they can only act when the donor actually loses capacity; this is often preferred where donors are concerned about preserving autonomy or minimising risk of financial abuse. The MCA 2005 accommodates both approaches, but the starting point remains that attorneys must follow the principles in section 1 and act in the donor's best interests.

In practice, drafting a Property and affairs LPA involves a balance between flexibility and control. A broadly drafted LPA gives attorneys the discretion they need to deal with situations that cannot be predicted in advance. However, instruments that are too open-ended can worry donors and increase the scope for disagreement or mistrust among family members, particularly where large sums of money or valuable assets are involved.

Effective drafting must also look ahead to the donor's likely future needs. A donor with significant investments may need attorneys with experience of managing portfolios and understanding financial risk. A donor who owns rental properties may require attorneys who can discharge the legal and practical responsibilities of a landlord. Where family relationships are complex—for example, in second marriages, blended families or situations involving estranged adult children—careful attorney selection and, where appropriate, supporting guidance can help reduce the risk of later conflict. In many cases, these considerations mean that the choice of attorney is ultimately more important than the detailed wording of the LPA itself.

2.2 Attorney Powers and Limits

Although a property and affairs LPA confers wide authority, that authority is carefully circumscribed by statute and cannot be expanded by the donor or the attorney. The Mental Capacity Act 2005 draws clear boundaries around what a property and affairs attorney may not do:

- First, an attorney's power to make gifts is strictly limited by section 12 MCA 2005. Attorneys may make only small, customary gifts on occasions such as birthdays, weddings or religious festivals, and charitable donations that the donor might reasonably have been expected to make. Any gift outside that narrow scope, whether by size, frequency or purpose, requires the approval of the Court of Protection. Case law has consistently treated unauthorised gifting as a serious breach of duty and a common basis for removal.

- Secondly, an attorney cannot make or amend a will on the donor's behalf. Testamentary decisions fall outside the scope of attorney authority and may only be made by the court through a statutory will under section 18(1)(i) MCA 2005. Any attempt by an attorney to influence succession planning without court approval risks being treated as an abuse of position.

- Third, some decisions are so personal that they can never be made by an attorney. An attorney cannot vote on the donor's behalf or exercise any political rights for them. These decisions must always be made by the individual themselves and cannot be delegated, even where the donor lacks capacity.[2]

Attorneys are also prohibited from delegating their authority. While they may take professional advice or instruct agents, for example solicitors, accountants or investment managers, the decision-making responsibility remains with the attorney. This reflects general fiduciary principles and is reinforced by the MCA Code of Practice (Chapter 7), which makes clear that attorneys must not abdicate their role.

Conflicts of interest are a further area of strict control. Attorneys may not benefit from their position or place themselves in a position of conflict unless the LPA expressly authorises it or the court gives approval. Self-dealing, preferential treatment or use of the donor's assets for the attorney's own benefit is incompatible with the duty to act in the donor's best interests under section 4 MCA 2005. The Court of Protection has repeatedly emphasised that even well-intentioned conflicts can justify intervention where they undermine trust or transparency.

2.3 Common Practice Issues

Several recurring issues emerge across practice:

- **Pressure from family members:** Attorneys may find themselves pressured by siblings, spouses or other relatives to distribute funds, make gifts, or take decisions that fall outside the statutory best interests test.

- **Capacity disputes:** There is often uncertainty over whether the donor has lost capacity for certain decisions, especially financial

[2] Section 29 MCA 2005

ones. Attorneys must follow the statutory test and may be criticised if they act prematurely.

- **Use of professional attorneys:** Increasingly, donors appoint solicitors, accountants or professional deputies as attorneys. This provides expertise but may raise cost concerns or create tension with family members.

- **Banks' response to LPAs:** Despite official guidance, financial institutions vary significantly in how they interpret and process LPAs. This inconsistent operational practice can complicate attorneys' roles.

Overall, the Property and affairs LPA remains the most widely used LPA type, reflecting the reality that financial incapacity is often the earliest practical manifestation of cognitive impairment. For that reason, these instruments continue to play a central role in both safeguarding donors and supporting families.

3. Health and Welfare LPAs

3.1 Purpose and Scope

A Health and Welfare LPA allows attorneys to make decisions about the donor's personal welfare, including where the donor lives, what care or support they receive, their day-to-day routine, and—if the donor has given express authority, decisions about life-sustaining treatment.

Unlike a property and affairs LPA, a Health and Welfare LPA can only be used once the donor lacks capacity to make the relevant decision. This is an express statutory safeguard set out in section 11(7) MCA 2005. Even where a Health and Welfare LPA exists, the attorney has no authority to act while the donor remains capable of deciding the matter for themselves.

This restriction reflects the core principles of the MCA 2005, particularly the presumption of capacity and the requirement that a person is not to be treated as unable to make a decision unless all practicable steps have been taken to help them do so (section 1(2)–(3)). Health and welfare decisions are often intensely personal and closely tied to an individual's dignity, identity and bodily integrity. Parliament has therefore drawn a clear line: decision-making authority does not pass to attorneys simply because an LPA exists, but only when capacity is lost in relation to the specific decision at hand.

As explained at paragraph 7.21 of the MCA 2005 Code of Practice, a Health and Welfare LPA may confer authority to make a wide range of personal welfare decisions:

> *LPAs can be used to appoint attorneys to make decisions about personal welfare, which can include healthcare and medical treatment decisions. Personal welfare LPAs might include decisions about:*
>
> - *where the donor should live and who they should live with*
> - *the donor's day-to-day care, including diet and dress*
> - *who the donor may have contact with*
> - *consenting to or refusing medical examination and treatment on the donor's behalf*
> - *arrangements needed for the donor to be given medical, dental or optical treatment*
> - *assessments for and provision of community care services*
> - *whether the donor should take part in social activities, leisure activities, education or training*

- *the donor's personal correspondence and papers*
- *rights of access to personal information about the donor*
- *complaints about the donor's care or treatment.*

The Health and Welfare LPA therefore operates across a wide range of settings, including community care, social work practice, mental health services, hospital treatment and decisions about moving into residential accommodation.

It is also arguable the type of LPA that engages directly with Convention rights under the European Convention on Human Rights, most notably Article 8 (respect for private and family life) and, where life-sustaining treatment decisions arise, Article 2 (the right to life).

3.2 Life-Sustaining Treatment Authority

The ability to grant attorneys power over life-sustaining treatment is distinctive. The donor must expressly choose to give this authority; it cannot be implied. This choice interacts with advance decisions to refuse treatment (ADRTs): if both exist, the most recent legally valid expression of the donor's wishes will take precedence.

The MCA 2005 thus creates a coherent hierarchy of planning instruments, but misunderstandings are common in practice. Attorneys must understand that even where they hold such authority, they must still apply the best interests test, taking into account the donor's wishes, values and beliefs. They cannot impose their own views about quality of life or medical treatment.

CHAPTER THREE

STRATEGIC APPLICATIONS FOR LPAs

1. Introduction

Lasting powers of attorney are often discussed as tools for managing personal finances and welfare. In practice, however, many donors hold roles and assets that sit well beyond the domestic sphere. Business ownership, professional practice, trust interests and international assets raise distinct legal and practical challenges that a standard property and financial affairs LPA may be ill-equipped to address.

This chapter explores how the LPA framework can be adapted to meet those challenges. It begins by examining Business LPAs: why they matter, how they differ from ordinary Property and affairs LPAs, and the particular risks that arise when incapacity intersects with commercial activity. It then turns to LPAs for complex estates, including trusts and cross-border assets, where questions of authority, recognition and coordination with other legal structures frequently arise.

Throughout, the emphasis is on functionality as well as validity. A carefully drafted LPA that cannot be operated in practice offers limited protection. Properly understood, LPAs in these contexts are not merely contingency documents but part of a broader strategy to preserve continuity, stability and confidence when capacity is lost.

2. Business LPAs

2.1 Why Business LPAs Matter

For business owners and individuals holding commercial or governance roles, loss of capacity raises risks that extend well beyond the management of private finances. Sole traders, partners, directors of owner-managed companies and professionals running regulated practices may find that incapacity immediately threatens the continued operation of the business itself. In practical terms, suppliers may go unpaid, payroll may be frozen, regulatory obligations unmet and contracts breached. In some sectors, incapacity can trigger intervention by a regulator or professional body, with potentially irreversible consequences for the business and those who depend upon it.

A standard property and financial affairs LPA is often an inadequate tool in this context. While it allows attorneys to manage personal finances, it may not confer sufficient or appropriate authority to run a trading entity, particularly where the business is subject to contractual, constitutional or regulatory constraints. Nor does it necessarily reflect the reality that the skills required to manage household bills, investments and property bear little resemblance to those required to oversee staff, cashflow, compliance and commercial risk.

Business LPAs respond to this gap by enabling donors to appoint attorneys specifically to manage business affairs, distinct from their personal financial arrangements. The separation of authority is not merely convenient but conceptually important. It allows the donor to tailor appointments to the nature of the business, to select attorneys with appropriate expertise, and to reduce the risk that personal and commercial interests become improperly entangled. The MCA 2005 framework permits this separation, and professional guidance has long recognised the legitimacy, and often the necessity, of keeping business and personal LPAs distinct

2.2 Key Features and Considerations

A Business LPA broadly mirrors the structure of a Property and affairs LPA but is carefully confined to business functions. Precision in drafting is essential. At a minimum, the instrument should clearly identify the business or businesses to which it relates, whether that is a sole trade, a partnership interest or a directorship within a company. Where the donor has multiple business interests, consideration should be given to whether a single Business LPA is appropriate or whether separate instruments are required to reflect different roles and risk profiles.

Attorney selection is particularly critical. The donor should consider not only trust and integrity, but also commercial competence and sector knowledge. An attorney who is perfectly capable of managing personal finances may be wholly unsuited to running a regulated practice, negotiating contracts or dealing with complex employment issues. Conversely, a business partner or co-director may be well placed to step in operationally but may not be appropriate to manage the donor's personal wealth.

Alignment with existing organisational documents is often the most overlooked, and most dangerous, aspect of Business LPA drafting:

- Partnership agreements, shareholders' agreements and articles of association frequently contain provisions restricting delegation, regulating decision-making, or specifying what happens on incapacity.

- For company directors, the Companies Act 2006 and the model articles permit delegation of powers, including by power of attorney, but also provide mechanisms by which a director may cease to hold office if certified as mentally incapable for a defined period.[3]

A Business LPA that purports to confer authority inconsistent with these documents risks being ineffective in practice, or worse, actively misleading.

Regulatory requirements must also be considered. In regulated professions, financial services, healthcare or other licensed sectors, authority to act may depend on holding specific qualifications or approvals. An attorney appointed under a Business LPA may not lawfully be able to carry out certain functions, regardless of what the instrument says. In such cases, the LPA may still be valuable in enabling high-level management decisions or transitional arrangements, but it cannot override statutory or regulatory constraints.

2.3 Managing Conflicts of Interest

Conflicts of interest are particularly acute in the business context. Attorneys appointed under a Business LPA are often shareholders, partners or fellow directors. Their personal commercial interests may align with the donor's in some respects but diverge sharply in others, especially where decisions affect remuneration, profit distribution, restructuring or exit strategies.

The general fiduciary principles applicable to attorneys under the MCA 2005 apply with equal force in business LPAs, but the commercial setting

---

[3] Model Article 18(e) provides that a person ceases to be a director if a registered medical practitioner who is treating that person gives a written opinion to the company stating that the person has become physically or mentally incapable of acting as a director and may remain so for more than three months. Many bespoke articles contain similar or even stricter provisions.

makes them harder to navigate. Attorneys must act in the donor's best interests, not their own, and must not allow personal or third-party interests to influence their decision-making.

Careful drafting can mitigate, though not eliminate, these risks. The LPA may include guidance, expressed in non-binding, precatory terms, about how conflicts should be identified and managed, when independent professional advice should be sought, and how decisions affecting both the donor and other stakeholders should be approached. Overly prescriptive or mandatory instructions risk invalidity, but well-crafted guidance can provide a valuable ethical and practical framework for attorneys operating under pressure.

2.4 Operational Realities

The effectiveness of a Business LPA is ultimately tested not by its legal validity but by its operability. Simply producing the registered instrument is rarely enough. Attorneys must be able to act quickly and decisively, often at a moment of crisis, to stabilise the business and reassure employees, clients and counterparties.

This requires practical access: to business bank accounts, payroll systems, accounting software, insurance policies, key contracts and regulatory correspondence. Financial institutions and counterparties may be cautious, particularly where the distinction between personal and business authority is unclear.

Best practice therefore extends beyond the LPA itself. Donors are well advised, while they retain capacity, to document key business processes, decision-making structures and lines of authority. A separate memorandum or business continuity document can sit alongside the Business LPA, providing attorneys with essential context without risking the validity of the instrument. Such preparatory work can make the difference between a temporary disruption and the collapse of an otherwise viable business.

In this sense, the Business LPA is not merely a legal safeguard but part of a broader resilience strategy. Properly conceived and drafted, it protects not only the donor, but also employees, clients and the wider commercial ecosystem that depends upon the continued functioning of the business.

3. LPAs for Complex Estates

3.1 Increasing Complexity in Modern Estates

The growth of international mobility, cross-border investments, dual residence, complex family structures and multi-jurisdictional wealth management means that LPAs increasingly operate within financially and legally complex landscapes. Donors may hold assets in multiple countries, benefit from settlements or offshore trusts, or operate through corporate structures. These arrangements raise a range of questions about the territorial reach of the LPA, recognition in foreign jurisdictions, and the scope of attorneys' authority.

3.2 Trusts and Attorneys

Where a donor is a beneficiary of a trust, particularly a discretionary trust, the attorney may still have an indirect role. The attorney may make personal financial decisions that are affected by trust distributions, such as budgeting, tax planning or use of income once it has been distributed to the donor. However, decisions about whether, when and how trust assets are distributed remain matters for the trustees. Attorneys cannot compel distributions, vary trust terms or exercise trustee discretions unless separately authorised.

This distinction reflects the separate legal nature of trusts. Trust property is not owned by the beneficiary personally, but is held by trustees subject to fiduciary duties owed to the class of beneficiaries as a whole. An attorney's authority is derived from the donor and extends only to the donor's personal property and affairs. It cannot displace or override the governance structure of a trust.

The position becomes more complex where the donor is themselves a trustee. Many trust deeds contain provisions dealing with incapacity, often providing for automatic removal, suspension or replacement of a trustee who lacks capacity. Incapacity may therefore trigger a change in trusteeship independently of the LPA regime. Even where the trust deed is silent, general trust law principles require trustees to have capacity to perform their duties, and incapacity will usually necessitate replacement.

In such cases, an attorney cannot simply "step into" the donor's role as trustee by virtue of the LPA. Separate mechanisms must be used, such as appointment under the trust instrument, reliance on statutory trustee replacement provisions, or an application to the court. Failure to recognise this distinction can lead to serious governance problems, including invalid trustee decisions or exposure to challenge by other trustees or beneficiaries.

3.3 Family Dynamics and High-Net-Worth Arrangements

Where large estates, complex wealth structures or significant business interests are involved, LPAs are particularly prone to dispute. The combination of valuable assets, family dynamics and loss of capacity often brings latent tensions to the surface. Decisions that might pass without comment in modest estates, such as transfers between accounts, investment strategy, or payment of family expenses, may attract close scrutiny where substantial sums are at stake.

Allegations commonly fall into familiar categories: that the donor was unduly influenced at the time the LPA was created; that attorneys are misusing funds or benefiting indirectly from their role; or that attorneys are acting in ways said to depart from the donor's true wishes, values or long-standing estate planning intentions. In high-value cases, disputes are often fuelled by inheritance expectations, blended families or historic grievances.

Strategic drafting can reduce, but not eliminate, these risks. Clear separation of personal and business authority, careful appointment of attorneys, use of replacement attorneys and well-expressed guidance about the donor's wishes can all help to manage expectations. Early communication with family members about the purpose and scope of the LPA may also reduce suspicion once the instrument comes into use. However, no drafting can fully insulate attorneys from challenge where significant assets are involved.

Court of Protection applications are also more common in high-value cases. These may include applications for directions on specific transactions, approval of gifts or tax planning, resolution of disputes between co-attorneys, or challenges to the validity or operation of the LPA itself. While such applications can be intrusive and costly, they also provide a mechanism for attorneys to obtain independent judicial approval, which may be particularly valuable where decisions are controversial or contested.

CHAPTER FOUR

DRAFTING AN EFFECTIVE LASTING POWER OF ATTORNEY

1. Introduction

Drafting a Lasting Power of Attorney may appear deceptively straightforward. The statutory forms are publicly available, the OPG encourages accessibility, and thousands of LPAs are registered each week without professional involvement. Yet the apparent simplicity masks significant legal, practical and interpersonal complexity. Poorly drafted LPAs can lead to disputes, safeguarding concerns, invalidity, or situations in which attorneys cannot act when needed. Conversely, a carefully prepared LPA can provide donors with security, family members with clarity and attorneys with the confidence that they are acting within the scope of their legal authority.

The task of drafting an effective LPA requires a balance between legal precision, foresight and sensitivity to the donor's personal circumstances. It demands an understanding of the statutory framework, familiarity with the practical realities of family dynamics and financial structures, and an ability to anticipate how decisions may unfold when the donor no longer has capacity.

This chapter explores the key elements of the drafting process: selecting attorneys and replacement attorneys; deciding between joint, joint and several or hybrid appointment structures; framing instructions and preferences; navigating lawful and unlawful wording; understanding the certificate provider's role; and ensuring correct execution to avoid registration defects. In doing so, it situates drafting not merely as a technical exercise but as a central aspect of safeguarding, autonomy and practical decision-making.

2. Selecting Attorneys and Replacement Attorneys

The selection of attorneys is the most significant and consequential decision a donor makes when creating a lasting power of attorney. The MCA 2005 affords donors wide autonomy in whom they appoint, but that freedom carries real responsibility. Attorneys are entrusted with decisions that may be financially complex, emotionally charged and taken at moments of crisis. Experience from Court of Protection litigation demonstrates that many of the most intractable disputes do not arise from defective drafting, but from poor choices at the point of appointment.

A recurring theme in practice is that donors underestimate both the weight of the role and the likelihood that relationships may deteriorate under pressure. Appointing an attorney is not an honorary position or a symbolic gesture of trust. It is the conferral of legal authority that may later be scrutinised by the Office of the OPG or the court, and, if exercised badly, may ultimately be revoked. Drafting an LPA without a careful, structured discussion about the suitability of each proposed attorney is one of the most common causes of later breakdown and litigation.

Professionals advising donors should therefore encourage a deliberate and reflective approach. The starting point is to consider the *nature of the decisions* the attorney will be required to make. An attorney does not need to be financially sophisticated, but they must be organised, financially literate and willing to seek advice when appropriate. For Health and Welfare LPAs, the demands are different but no less significant. Attorneys may need to engage confidently with clinicians and social workers and navigate complex care systems.

Not all donors appreciate these distinctions at the outset. Many default to appointing a spouse or adult child without pausing to consider whether that person has the emotional resilience, time or temperament to perform the role. A loving relationship does not necessarily translate into effective decision-making, particularly where guilt, denial or family pressure may impair judgement.

Interpersonal dynamics between attorneys are equally critical. Families are rarely as harmonious as donors hope, and existing fault lines are often exposed rather than healed by shared authority. Appointing siblings with a history of rivalry or unresolved conflict is frequently a recipe for paralysis or dispute. The pressure of acting under an LPA, often in circumstances of declining health or crisis, tends to magnify, rather than soften, existing tensions. Donors should be encouraged to appoint individuals who communicate well, respect boundaries and can act collaboratively in the donor's best interests, even where they disagree personally.

Geographical considerations also deserve careful attention. Although many tasks can now be performed remotely, physical distance can still complicate practical matters such as managing property, attending care reviews or dealing with local professionals. Attorneys who live abroad may face delays, logistical difficulties and increased scrutiny from banks and other institutions, some of which are reluctant to deal with non-UK resident attorneys. These factors should be discussed openly at the drafting stage, rather than discovered later in the midst of an emergency.

Replacement attorneys are an essential, but frequently overlooked, component of effective planning. Without replacement provisions, an LPA may fail entirely if an original attorney dies, loses capacity, becomes bankrupt or is otherwise unable to act. The absence of a replacement can force unnecessary applications to the Court of Protection, with associated delay, cost and stress. Replacement attorneys need not be as actively involved at the outset, but they must nonetheless be suitable, willing and capable of stepping into the role if required. Drafting should make clear whether replacements act jointly, jointly and severally, or in a defined order, to avoid uncertainty at the point of transition.

Experience from contested cases shows that removing an unsuitable attorney is rarely quick, cheap or emotionally contained. Applications to revoke an LPA can involve investigation by the Office of the OPG, contested hearings, fact-finding and significant costs, often borne by the donor's estate. The best safeguard against such outcomes is careful selection at the outset.

Ultimately, choosing attorneys is an exercise in anticipating future vulnerability, both the donor's and the attorneys'. The most effective drafting conversations are frank, empathetic and grounded in realism, rather than optimism. Time spent selecting the right people, and putting appropriate replacement structures in place, is often the single most important investment a donor can make in the long-term effectiveness of their LPA.

3. Joint or Joint and Several Appointments

Once attorneys have been selected, donors must decide how they are to act. The MCA 2005 offers two basic structural models: attorneys may be appointed to act jointly, or jointly and severally. Although this choice is sometimes treated as a technical drafting point, it in fact reflects a fundamental philosophy about trust, risk and decision-making. The structure chosen will often determine whether an LPA functions smoothly in practice or becomes a source of delay, dispute or eventual court intervention.

3.1 Joint appointment

Under a joint appointment, attorneys must agree unanimously on every decision within the scope of the LPA. Donors are often drawn to this model because it appears to offer a strong safeguard. Requiring unanimity can feel reassuring, particularly where substantial assets are involved or where the donor fears that one attorney might act impulsively or without proper consultation. In theory, joint decision-making promotes accountability, transparency and shared responsibility.

In practice, however, joint appointment is frequently rigid and fragile. The LPA depends on all attorneys remaining available, cooperative and capable. If one attorney becomes uncontactable, disengaged, seriously ill, bankrupt or loses capacity, the entire appointment may grind to a halt. Even short-term absence or delay can prevent urgent action, for example where bills must be paid, care arrangements need to be put in place, or time-sensitive financial decisions arise. Where relationships between attorneys deteriorate, unanimity can quickly become impossible, leaving the donor's affairs effectively frozen.

For these reasons, joint appointment tends to be appropriate only in limited circumstances. It may be suitable where the donor anticipates infrequent but high-risk decisions, such as the sale of a unique or valuable asset, or a one-off business transaction, and where the attorneys are demonstrably able to work collaboratively. As a general structure for ongoing management, however, it is often too inflexible to withstand the realities of long-term incapacity.

3.2 Joint and several appointment

Joint and several appointment offers a markedly different approach. Each attorney may act independently, without the consent or knowledge of the others. This structure prioritises flexibility and responsiveness. It allows decisions to be taken quickly, avoids bottlenecks and ensures that the donor's affairs can continue even if one attorney becomes unavailable. For this reason, it is the model most commonly recommended in practice, particularly where attorneys trust one another and communicate well.

That flexibility comes at a price. Joint and several appointment increases the scope for disagreement between attorneys and, in the worst cases, for unilateral action that others would not have supported. One attorney may pursue a course of action, such as selling an asset or changing investment strategy, that another considers imprudent or contrary to the donor's wishes. Although attorneys remain subject to fiduciary duties and the best-interests framework, disputes of this kind can be deeply destabilising and may ultimately require intervention by the Court of Protection.

Donors should therefore be encouraged to think carefully about the personal dynamics involved. Joint and several appointment works best where attorneys have a shared understanding of the donor's values and a genuine willingness to consult one another, even if not legally required to do so. Including clear preferences or guidance within the LPA can help reinforce the donor's expectation that attorneys will act collaboratively and keep one another informed.

3.3 Hybrid structures

Hybrid appointment structures attempt to balance these competing considerations. Under a hybrid model, attorneys are required to act jointly for certain categories of decision, but may act jointly and severally for others. A common example is requiring joint decision-making for the sale of property, major investments or transactions above a specified financial threshold, while allowing joint and several authority for routine financial management such as paying bills or managing day-to-day expenditure.

Hybrids can be particularly effective where donors appoint a mix of family members and professional attorneys. They allow everyday matters to be dealt with efficiently, while ensuring that significant or irreversible decisions benefit from collective scrutiny and, where appropriate, professional oversight. When well drafted, hybrid structures can reduce both the risk of paralysis and the risk of unchecked unilateral action.

However, hybrid arrangements demand careful drafting. The categories of decision that require joint action must be defined with sufficient clarity to be workable in practice. Overly detailed or convoluted distinctions can create uncertainty, delay and disagreement among attorneys, and may undermine the effectiveness of the LPA. There is also a risk that overly prescriptive instructions stray into mandatory territory or create internal inconsistency.

Donors should therefore be encouraged to focus on what truly matters to them. Rather than attempting to anticipate every possible scenario, the aim should be to establish a clear and intelligible framework that reflects the donor's priorities and risk tolerance. The LPA is not a commercial contract or a contingency manual. Its purpose is to provide a durable and adaptable structure within which trusted individuals can make decisions in the donor's best interests as circumstances evolve.

4. Instructions and Preferences: Lawful, Unlawful and Problematic Wording

The preferences and instructions section of an LPA offers donors an important opportunity to articulate their values, expectations and priorities. Used well, it can provide attorneys with crucial context when applying the best interests test and help ensure that decisions reflect the donor's sense of self. Used poorly, however, it is one of the most common sources of difficulty in both registration and later operation of LPAs. Incorrect, unlawful or unclear wording can lead to refusal or delay in registration, severance of clauses, or disputes that ultimately require court intervention.

The distinction between preferences and instructions is therefore central. Preferences are non-binding statements of wish or belief. They do not direct outcomes, but guide attorneys in exercising their discretion and applying the statutory best interests framework. Typical examples include:

- expressions of religious or cultural practice,
- dietary preferences,
- attitudes to medical treatment,
- views about remaining at home, or
- hopes about how family relationships should be managed.

Preferences should be framed flexibly, recognising that circumstances may change. Their function is to act as a compass, not a set of fixed directions.

Instructions, by contrast, are binding. Attorneys are legally required to follow them unless doing so would be unlawful or impossible. Because instructions constrain discretion, they must be drafted with particular care. Instructions that cut across the MCA 2005 are invalid. Common examples include directions that require gifts beyond the narrow scope permitted by section 12 MCA 2005, or mandate outcomes that prevent attorneys from applying the best interests test. Where such provisions are included, the Office of the OPG may refuse registration or apply to the Court of Protection for severance.

The risks associated with over-prescriptive drafting were examined in detail in *Re Various Lasting Powers of Attorney* [2019] EWCOP 40, a case in which the Senior Judge considered a number of LPAs containing extensive instructions and conditions imposed by donors. The donors' intentions were generally benign: they sought to control how attorneys made decisions, to allocate responsibilities between different attorneys or to require consultation with professionals or family members. However, many of the provisions were framed in mandatory terms that purported to bind attorneys in ways incompatible with the statutory scheme.

The court reaffirmed that while donors are entitled to express wishes and preferences, they cannot use the instructions section to dictate how attorneys must reach decisions or to fetter their statutory discretion. Instructions expressed in mandatory language, such as “must”, “shall” or “only if”, were particularly problematic where they attempted to: allocate decision-making authority to third parties; impose fixed decision-making hierarchies not recognised by the Act; or require attorneys to act in a way that might conflict with best interests. The court held that such provisions could not form part of a valid LPA and were liable to be severed.

Crucially, the judgment drew a clear distinction between binding instructions and non-binding guidance. The court emphasised that wording expressed in precatory terms, for example, “I would like”, “I wish”, or “I would prefer”, may be effective as a written statement of the donor’s wishes, even if it cannot operate as a binding instruction. Such statements can properly inform attorneys’ decision-making and may carry significant weight in best interests assessments, without unlawfully constraining discretion. The problem in the cases before the court was not that donors sought to give guidance, but that they attempted to do so in mandatory terms that purported to control outcomes rather than inform judgement.

This distinction has important practical consequences. Instructions that seek to prohibit certain actions outright, such as a blanket ban on selling the donor’s home, or a requirement to follow the views of a particular family member, are especially vulnerable. So too are provisions that mandate particular investment strategies, require consent from third parties, or direct attorneys to prioritise the donor’s stated wishes even where circumstances have changed. Although often motivated by a desire to preserve autonomy or prevent family conflict, such provisions frequently undermine the statutory framework and increase the likelihood of registration difficulties or later litigation.

In practice, donors are usually better served by reframing rigid instructions as preferences. For example, an instruction stating, "My attorneys must never sell my home," can be re-expressed as, "I would prefer to remain in my home for as long as reasonably possible, and I would like my attorneys to explore all available options to support this before considering a sale." This approach preserves the donor's voice and values while allowing attorneys to respond lawfully and flexibly to future circumstances.

More specialist drafting may be required where donors have complex arrangements, such as reliance on trust income, substantial investment portfolios, or sensitive family dynamics. In such cases, it may be preferable to place detailed guidance in a separate memorandum of wishes rather than on the LPA form itself. This avoids the risk of invalidity while still providing attorneys with meaningful direction.

Ultimately, the preferences and instructions section is most effective when it communicates principles rather than prescriptions. Donors should be encouraged to articulate what matters to them and why, rather than attempting to dictate future decisions in detail. Properly framed, preferences can exert real influence over attorney decision-making while remaining consistent with the MCA 2005 and the approach endorsed by the Senior Judge.

5. Certificate Providers and Safeguarding Considerations

5.1 An important safeguard

The certificate provider is one of the most significant safeguards built into the LPA regime. Their function is not administrative, nor is it merely confirmatory. They operate as a protective gatekeeper at the point of execution, tasked with ensuring that the donor understands what they are doing, that they are acting freely and voluntarily, and that there is no fraud, coercion or other factor that would undermine the legitimacy of the appointment. In many respects, the certificate provider is the only independent safeguard at the moment when authority is irrevocably transferred to another person.

This safeguarding role is reflected both in statute and in guidance. The LPA instrument itself requires the certificate provider to certify that, at the time of execution, the donor understood the purpose of the LPA and the scope of the authority conferred; that no fraud or undue pressure was being used to induce the donor to create it; and that there was nothing else that would prevent the LPA from being validly made. These are not formulaic declarations. Each goes to the heart of voluntariness and capacity, and together they impose a serious professional and ethical responsibility on the individual signing the certificate.

The current model represents a deliberate policy choice. During the development of the MCA 2005, the Law Commission considered more onerous safeguards, including mandatory certification by both a doctor and a solicitor, and drew on comparative models from jurisdictions such as Quebec, Ontario and Scotland, where professional attestation plays a central role. Ultimately, concerns about cost, accessibility and practicality led to the adoption of a single certificate provider model. That decision places considerable weight on the judgement and integrity of the individual chosen. It also explains why the role must be approached as a substantive assessment, not a procedural step.

Where donors are vulnerable, the certificate provider's role becomes even more acute. Vulnerability can arise from a range of factors including early cognitive impairment, physical frailty, emotional dependence, financial reliance, social isolation or entrenched family dynamics, each of which can obscure whether the donor truly understands the document they are signing or is acting freely. In vulnerable cases, warning signs may include hesitancy or confusion when naming attorneys, inconsistent explanations of the purpose of the LPA, visible anxiety, or repeated references to what another person wants rather than what the donor wants. Deference to a dominant family member, particularly one who stands to benefit from the appointment, should prompt careful scrutiny.

In such situations, the certificate provider may need to pause the process, seek further information, or decline to sign. Declining to provide a certificate is not an accusation of wrongdoing; it is a legitimate exercise of the safeguarding responsibility Parliament intended when it introduced the certificate requirement.

The Court of Protection decision in *TA v The OPG* [2023] EWCOP 63 underlines this point forcefully. In that case, the donor executed two LPAs appointing her daughter as sole attorney for both property and financial affairs and health and welfare. The certificate provider, a friend and former family relation, signed the certificates, but later evidence gathered by a OPG investigation revealed that she had done little more than ask the donor if she was "happy about it" and accepted a positive answer. There was no detailed engagement to ensure that the donor understood the purpose and scope of the instrument, that no undue pressure was being exerted, or that there were no other barriers to the creation of the LPA. The certificate provider did not obtain or appear to form a considered opinion on the three statutory matters she was required to certify. As a result, the Court found the certificates invalid and the LPAs of no effect.

The reasoning in *TA v The OPG* is particularly instructive. Lieven J affirmed that the statutory requirement is not satisfied by a mere signature on a certificate form: the certificate provider must form an actual opinion about the donor's understanding, voluntariness and absence of barriers to creation, and be able to explain how that opinion was reached. The Court held that the certificate must have "particular content", that is, it must genuinely reflect that the certificate provider has engaged their mind with the matters in paragraph 2(1)(e) of Schedule 1 to the MCA 2005. The mere existence of a certificate in the correct form cannot be taken as conclusive evidence that the donor properly understood the instrument or was free from undue influence.

This decision has two principal implications for vulnerable donors and those who assist them.

- First, it reinforces that the certificate provider must do more than a superficial check: they must actively assess whether the donor comprehends what they are signing and is acting voluntarily. Asking a donor "Are you happy with this?" is unlikely to suffice. Instead, the certificate provider should engage in a supportive but probing discussion, covering the purpose of the LPA, the identity and role of the attorneys, and any circumstances that might suggest pressure or misunderstanding.

- Second, the decision illustrates that courts will treat the certificate provider's evidence as central if the validity of an LPA is later challenged. Good contemporaneous record-keeping is therefore crucial. Professionals should document the questions asked, the donor's responses, and the reasoning that led them to conclude that the statutory criteria were met. This is especially important where capacity is borderline or family relationships appear strained; an attendance note may be the only evidence available years later if the certificate provider is unavailable or cannot recall details. Without such records, the LPA may be vulnerable to challenge on the basis that the safeguards Parliament built into the certification process were not actually engaged.

5.2 Who can give a certificate?

Certificate providers must fall within one of two categories: either someone who has known the donor personally for at least two years, or someone with relevant professional skills who reasonably considers themselves competent to make the required judgements. The certificate provider must be someone whose sole role is to protect the donor's interests, not to facilitate the wishes of attorneys or family members.

The choice between a "lay" certificate provider and a professional one is therefore significant. Family friends or acquaintances who have known the donor socially may be well placed to notice changes over time and may feel trusted by the donor. However, they may lack the skills to identify subtle cognitive impairment, relational pressure or financial coercion, particularly where these present in nuanced or socially masked ways. Professionals, such as solicitors, barristers, doctors or social workers, bring experience of assessing capacity and voluntariness, and may be better equipped to recognise red flags. That said, donors may feel less comfortable speaking candidly with professionals, particularly where family relationships are sensitive or dependency is involved. There is no universally "right" choice, but donors should be advised that the robustness of the safeguard depends heavily on who is selected.

For professionals acting as certificate providers, the requirement to meet the donor privately is critical. This conversation must take place without attorneys, relatives or carers present. It is often the only opportunity for the donor to speak freely, and its importance cannot be overstated. The discussion should explore, in an open and supportive way, the donor's understanding of the LPA, including who the attorneys are, what powers they will have, when those powers will take effect, and the fact that the appointment may operate for many years. The provider should also test whether the donor appreciates that the LPA can be difficult to undo, and that attorneys may one day make decisions the donor would not have anticipated.

5.3 Who can't give certificate?

Regulation 8 of the Lasting Powers of Attorney, Enduring Powers of Attorney and OPG Regulations 2007 specifies categories of person who are disqualified from acting as a certificate provider in respect of any instrument intended to create a lasting power of attorney. These provisions operate alongside the general eligibility requirements (such as the two-year personal knowledge test or relevant professional competence) to ensure that the certificate provider can genuinely attest to the donor's understanding and voluntariness without conflict or undue influence.

Regulation 8 disqualifications include:

- **Family members of the donor**

  A person cannot act as certificate provider if they are a member of the donor's family. This reflects the risk that close family relationships might carry implicit pressures or loyalties that could compromise independent judgment.

- **A donee of the lasting power of attorney**

  Anyone who is, or will be, appointed as an attorney under the LPA cannot serve as certificate provider for that same instrument. This includes multiple attorneys where the donor has appointed more than one person. The rationale is straightforward: an attorney stands to benefit directly from the instrument and cannot be expected to verify the donor's free and informed consent impartially.

- **A donee under another lasting or enduring power of attorney executed by the donor**

  A person who is already appointed as an attorney under a different instrument made by the donor, whether another LPA or an enduring power of attorney, may not act as certificate provider. This prevents conflicts arising from overlapping roles and avoids placing the certificate provider in a position of self-verification.

- **Family members of a done**

  The disqualification extends beyond the attorney themselves to their family members. The logic is that familial ties to an attorney could create similar pressures or dependencies that undermine independence.

- **Independent Mental Capacity Advocates (IMCAs)**

  Individuals acting in a statutory advocacy role under the Mental Capacity Act are expressly excluded from acting as certificate providers. Although IMCAs are independent, their statutory functions are distinct from the certification role, and mixing these roles could compromise both safeguarding functions.

- **Additional categories**

  While Regulation 8(3) sets out the principal disqualifications, practice guidance from the Office of the OPG and professional bodies usually interprets these categories expansively to include persons whose independence might reasonably be questioned, for example, carers, care-home staff, business partners or employees of the donor, or persons connected through financial or professional dependency. Professional practice guidance emphasises that the disqualifications must be understood purposively, focusing on substantive independence rather than formal labels.

Understanding these disqualifications is crucial in practice. An otherwise willing and trusted friend who falls into one of the above categories cannot lawfully certify an LPA. Failure to comply with Regulation 8 not only undermines the protective purpose of the certificate provider but can render the LPA invalid.

From a drafting perspective, donors and advisers should therefore check carefully whether a proposed certificate provider falls into any disallowed category before execution. Where relationships are complex or professional boundaries uncertain (for example, longstanding carers, "trusted advisers" who are also friends, or business associates), it may be necessary to select an alternative.

6. Witnessing an LPA

Under Schedule 1 to the MCA 2005, an LPA must be executed in prescribed form and with proper witnessing of signatures. Each person who signs the LPA must do so in the physical presence of a witness, who then attests to that signature. Electronic or remote witnessing (for example by video link) does not satisfy this requirement; the witness must actually observe the signatory sign the document in person.

All witnesses must be at least 18 years old, and they must be capable of understanding the significance of attesting to the signature. While family members and friends may often serve as witnesses, there are important limitations on who can act as a valid witness for particular signatures.

The rules governing who may witness signatures on an LPA seek to preserve the impartiality and independence of the attestation process. In particular:

- Attorneys named in the LPA may not witness the donor's signature. This is a mandatory rule. A donee (attorney) or replacement attorney is expressly disallowed from witnessing the donor's signature, even if the attorney is otherwise an eligible adult witness.

- The donor themselves may not witness an attorney's signature. Likewise, a donor cannot serve as witness to another party's signature on the LPA.

- There is no absolute bar on attorneys witnessing one another's signatures, but caution is advisable from a formalities perspective to avoid confusion or challenge.

These rules reflect both statutory prescription and judicial interpretation. The prohibition on attorneys witnessing the donor's signature is not an optional or advisory rule; it is a mandatory condition of proper execution.

If the formal requirements are not met, the instrument may have no legal effect at all.

The importance of these witnessing rules was starkly illustrated in *Office of the OPG v PGO & Ors (Re BGO)* [2019] EWCOP 13. In that case, an 84-year-old donor executed two LPAs, one for property and financial affairs and one for health and welfare. However, a financial institution later noted that the donor's signature on the property and financial affairs LPA had been witnessed by one of the proposed attorneys.

The Office of the OPG applied to the Court of Protection for a declaration as to whether the formal requirements had been met. The court observed that:

- Schedule 1 of the MCA 2005 requires that LPAs be executed in accordance with the prescribed formalities, including proper witnessing of signatures, and that the OPG must cancel the registration if these requirements have not been satisfied.
- Relevant subordinate regulations (Regulation 9(8)(b) of the Lasting Powers of Attorney, Enduring Powers of Attorney and OPG Regulations 2007) expressly provide that a donee may not witness any required signature except that of another donee.
- Because one of the attorneys had witnessed the donor's signature contrary to this rule, the requirements of execution had not been met. The judge held that these requirements are mandatory and that the court "had no choice" but to direct cancellation of the registration of both LPAs.

The outcome in BGO had significant practical consequences. By the time the defect was discovered, the donor had lost capacity and could no longer execute new LPAs to cure the defect. The court observed with regret that the donor's intention to empower trusted attorneys could not be given effect because of a seemingly straightforward error in execution, and that the only available recourse was an application for a deputy to be appointed.

7. Execution Formalities and Avoiding Registration Defects

Even the most carefully drafted LPA can falter if execution formalities are not observed. The MCA 2005 and associated regulations impose a strict order of signing: the donor signs first, the certificate provider signs second, and the attorneys sign last. Each signature must be correctly dated. Any deviation risks invalidity or registration failure.

Common registration defects include:

- mismatch in dates—for example, attorneys signing before the certificate provider
- inconsistent ink or handwriting suggesting retrospective dating
- missing signatures, particularly in replacement attorney sections;
- contradictory appointment structures;
- witnessing errors;
- incomplete pages or missing continuation sheets.

Professional supervision of execution significantly reduces these risks. Donors should sign in the presence of an independent witness, ensuring clarity about identity and voluntariness. Attorneys may sign their sections separately, but witnesses must again be physically present. While electronic signatures remain impermissible for LPAs, future reform proposals may revisit this requirement (discussed in Chapter Nine).

The OPG examines each LPA closely during registration. Although it can return documents for correction, certain defects, particularly those involving execution order, cannot be remedied. This creates distress for donors who may already be losing capacity and can lead to costly and time-consuming deputyship applications. Avoiding these errors is therefore not merely an administrative matter but a core aspect of safeguarding the donor's future autonomy.

Practitioners should maintain detailed records of the execution process, including the identity of witnesses and circumstances of signing. Clear documentation helps resolve later queries and demonstrates adherence to best practice.

CHAPTER FIVE

CAPACITY TO MAKE AN LPA

1. Introduction

The question of whether a person has the mental capacity to create a Lasting Power of Attorney lies at the heart of the statutory scheme. LPAs derive their legitimacy from the donor's autonomous act of appointment; without valid capacity at the point of execution, the document fails entirely.

This chapter explores the statutory principles that govern capacity to make an LPA, the complexities of borderline capacity, the importance of evidential safeguards, the challenges posed by undue influence and the professional responsibilities that arise when legal practitioners, healthcare professionals and certificate providers participate in the LPA process.

2. The capacity test

2.1 Capacity to create a Lasting Power of Attorney

Someone's capacity to create an LPA may be scrutinised at different stages of the process:

- when a solicitor is first advising on whether an LPA should be made;
- when the donor signs the completed document;
- when an attorney later seeks to use the registered LPA; and

- if a disagreement arises about the validity of the instrument or how an attorney is exercising their powers.

At each of these points, the question of capacity is approached using the statutory test in the MCA 2005. Since April 2007, the MCA has provided the definitive legal framework. Although the Act says that its definition applies "for the purposes of this Act," the earlier common-law authorities remain relevant in interpreting what that definition requires. The courts therefore apply the MCA test through the lens of the existing jurisprudence, and long-established common-law principles, especially those concerned with the level of understanding needed and the importance of focusing on the salient facts, continue to shape the assessment.

I do not repeat here the statutory test for capacity under the MCA. What distinguishes a decision to execute an LPA from many other decisions is the specific information the donor must be able to understand, retain, and use or weigh.[4] That information will necessarily vary depending on the individual and their circumstances.[5] However, in *OPG v RI & Ors* [2022] EWCOP 22, Poole J confirmed that, in order to have capacity to execute an LPA, a donor should be able to appreciate:

- **The purpose and effect of the LPA**. That it gives chosen individuals authority to make decisions on the donor's behalf in the future.

- **The identity of the proposed attorney**(s) and the significance of entrusting those individuals with decision-making powers.

- **The range and limits of the attorney's authority**, including the constraints set by the MCA 2005 and the LPA document itself.

---

4 Section 3 MCA 2005

5 *A Local Authority v JB* [2021] UKSC 52

- **When those powers can be exercised**, including the need for registration with the OPG and the fact that some decisions only arise when the donor lacks capacity.

- **The types of decisions and assets** the attorney will be able to manage.

- **The donor's continuing ability to revoke the LPA** while they remain capacitous.

- **The main advantages and disadvantages** of making this particular LPA and of choosing not to.

Importantly, the courts stress that the threshold must not be pitched unrealistically high. A donor need not comprehend every clause or foresee every possible outcome. The exercise demands an understanding of the *salient information*, not a mastery of legal detail. As earlier authorities have put it[6], the relevant standard mirrors what would ordinarily be expected of any member of the public making this kind of decision: a broad, practical grasp of the essentials, rather than a lawyer's level of precision.

This approach balances respect for personal autonomy with the protective function of the MCA, ensuring that donors can make meaningful, personal choices about their future while preventing capacity from being assessed against an unnecessarily exacting standard.

2.2 Capacity to revoke a Lasting Power of Attorney

Just as the creation of an LPA is a significant act, so too is its revocation. A donor may bring an LPA to an end at any point, even after registration, provided they have the mental capacity to make that decision. The focus

---

6 *CC v KK & STCC* [2012] EWCOP 2136

is again on whether the donor can understand, retain and use the relevant information for that choice when these are explained appropriately.

In broad terms, the donor must be able to grasp[7]:

- **Who the attorney(s) are**, and the role they currently play.
- **What powers the attorney(s) hold**, and the scope of their authority under the existing LPA.
- **Why ending the arrangement is being considered**, and the reasons it may be necessary or sensible to do so.
- **The likely consequences of revocation**, including the loss of the attorney's authority and any practical impact on the donor's decision-making arrangements.

The safest and most formal way to revoke it is through a deed of revocation. A deed provides clarity, proof and a single point of reference for the OPG and for third parties.

If the donor lacks capacity to revoke an LPA, the Court of Protection has power to intervene. In appropriate circumstances, the court may revoke an existing LPA on the donor's behalf, particularly where an attorney is acting improperly or where the arrangement no longer accords with the donor's best interests (discussed further in Chapter Seven).

2.3 Practical steps to support a decision

Section 1(3) of the MCA 2005 requires that a person is not to be treated as unable to make a decision unless all practicable steps have been taken

7 This list again draws on *OPG v RI & Ors* [2022] EWCOP 22

to help them to do so, without success. This principle is central to the assessment of a donor's capacity to create a lasting power of attorney.

The task is not confined to testing comprehension in the abstract. It requires practitioners to take active steps to enable the donor to engage with the decision in a way that reflects their own abilities and circumstances.

Unlike the Mental Capacity Act (Northern Ireland) 2016, which provides a detailed and prescriptive account of what constitutes support for decision-making[8], what amounts to "all practicable steps" in England and Wales will depend on the individual. This may include simplifying language, using visual or written aids, repeating information, breaking the decision into manageable elements, allowing time and rest breaks, adapting communication methods, or involving an advocate or trusted third party where appropriate. Such steps may be decisive in enabling a donor to understand, retain, use and weigh the relevant information sufficiently to make the decision for themselves.

At the same time, section 1(3) does not permit capacity to be assumed through excessive assistance. The decision must ultimately be the donor's. If the level of intervention required goes beyond enabling understanding and instead risks compensating for an inability to make the decision, the statutory test will not be met. Practitioners must therefore strike a careful balance between taking all practicable steps to assist and ensuring that the donor is genuinely making the decision for themselves.

2.4 Borderline Capacity and Evidential Requirements

Borderline capacity is one of the most challenging areas for practitioners. Many donors seeking to create LPAs do so in the early stages of dementia,

---

8 Section 5

or during periods of cognitive fluctuation or when their cognitive abilities begin to decline. These situations require careful, nuanced assessment. The law recognises that capacity may vary from day to day or even within a single day; a donor may have capacity in the morning but lack it by afternoon. This fluidity demands flexibility, patience and careful timing.

Where capacity is borderline, the assessment must be particularly robust. Practitioners should document the donor's understanding in detail, noting the questions asked, the donor's responses, the support provided and the practitioner's reasoning. The certificate provider plays a vital role here, but the responsibility does not fall on them alone. If a solicitor, financial adviser or healthcare professional participates in drafting or preparation, they too have a duty to ensure that the donor understands the decision. Family members too may be invited to document their contemporaneous impression of the person in a file note or similar.

Medical evidence is not mandatory, but it is often prudent. A GP or social worker assessment can be invaluable where cognitive impairment is suspected or where family tensions make later disputes likely. The Court of Protection increasingly expects evidence where a donor displays clear vulnerabilities. While professionals must avoid unnecessary medicalisation of capacity, they should not hesitate to seek expert input when capacity is unclear.

Borderline capacity can be hard to spot. A donor may speak confidently and seem to understand what is being discussed, but still struggle to weigh risks or think ahead. They may understand what is happening now, but not what could happen in the future. Documenting the assessment and interaction is therefore essential. If disputes arise, contemporaneous notes provide the strongest evidence of voluntariness and understanding. The absence of proper records may expose the LPA to challenge and undermine confidence in the process.

3. When to Refuse to Act as Drafter or Certificate Provider

There are circumstances in which professionals must decline to act. This is not a failure but a positive fulfilment of their safeguarding responsibilities. Where capacity is doubtful or the donor cannot be adequately supported to understand the decision, refusing to proceed is the correct legal and ethical course.

Refusing to act may be necessary when the donor cannot explain the purpose of the LPA, is unaware of the powers being given, or cannot identify reasons for choosing particular attorneys. It may also be required where the donor's understanding fluctuates to the extent that no stable period of capacity can be identified, or where the dynamics of coercion are so strong that voluntariness cannot be established.

Declining to act should be handled sensitively. Donors should be informed of the reasons, provided with clear explanations, and directed towards alternative options, such as obtaining a medical assessment or involving local safeguarding bodies. Where appropriate, professionals may suggest considering a deputyship application if the donor is unable to execute an LPA but still requires support.

Documentation is essential. Detailed notes should be kept of the concerns, the steps taken to support the donor, and the reasons for refusing to proceed. These records may become important evidence in later disputes or safeguarding investigations.

CHAPTER SIX

INTERACTION WITH OTHER LEGAL AND MEDICAL INSTRUMENTS

1. Introduction

The creation and use of Lasting Powers of Attorney never occur in a vacuum. LPAs sit within a dense ecosystem of legal, financial and medical instruments, each carrying its own logic, hierarchy and operational framework. Attorneys must navigate these overlapping structures with care, and practitioners advising donors may need to understand how LPAs interact with deputyships, advance decisions to refuse treatment, trust arrangements, co-ownership issues, business governance documents and estate planning. This chapter explores these intersections and provides a foundation for understanding how LPAs operate alongside other legal mechanisms.

2. Deputyships and LPAs

Deputyship and LPAs represent two distinct routes to substituted decision-making under the MCA 2005. LPAs reflect an anticipatory exercise of autonomy: the donor chooses attorneys while they still have capacity. Deputyships arise when no valid or workable LPA exists and the Court of Protection must appoint someone to act. The two instruments share many structural features, both involve substituted decision-making and must apply the best interests framework, but they differ in origin, scope, supervision and judicial oversight.

Where a valid and operative LPA exists, the Court of Protection will rarely appoint a deputy. The statutory scheme reflects a strong presumption that the donor's own choice of decision-maker should be respected, and section 20(4) of the MCA 2005 expressly prevents the court from conferring on a deputy any power that would be inconsistent with a decision made, within the scope of their authority and in accordance with the Act, by an attorney appointed under a lasting power of attorney. In practice, this significantly limits the circumstances in which a deputyship will be appropriate where an LPA is in place.

However, deputyships remain relevant in several situations. First, an LPA may be defective or invalid, for example because of execution errors, improper witnessing, revoked or impermissible instructions, or a successful objection to registration. Second, attorneys may be unwilling, unable or unsuitable to act, whether due to illness, bankruptcy, conflict of interest or lack of engagement. Third, even where attorneys are acting competently and within their authority, the Court may still appoint a deputy for discrete matters that fall outside the scope of the LPA or require judicial oversight, particularly in complex property and affairs cases, provided that the deputy's powers do not cut across decisions lawfully made by the attorney.

Deputyships also intersect with LPAs when donors have created only one type of LPA. For instance, a donor with a Property and Financial Affairs LPA may later lose capacity to make health and welfare decisions without having created a Health and Welfare LPA. In such cases, the Court may appoint a welfare deputy, although in practice welfare deputyships remain rare and are granted only in exceptional circumstances.

Practitioners must also consider the possibility of hybrid systems where attorneys and deputies act concurrently for different areas of decision-making. This can create tension. Attorneys may hold authority for financial matters while a deputy is appointed to make decisions about a specific property sale or litigation settlement. Clear communication and careful role delineation are essential to avoid conflicts or duplication.

From a practitioner's perspective, the existence of an LPA should not be treated as a complete bar to deputyship. Instead, the question should be framed around whether the attorneys can adequately exercise the donor's wishes and best interests in the particular circumstances. Where they cannot, the court has flexibility to intervene, supplement or replace the LPA structure.

3. Advance decisions

Advance decisions to refuse treatment (ADRTs) sit alongside, but separate from, Health and Welfare LPAs under the Mental Capacity Act 2005. If an ADRT is valid and applies to the situation at hand, doctors must follow it. It is legally binding and does not depend on what others think is best.

How an ADRT interacts with a Health and Welfare LPA depends mainly on which document was made last:

- If a donor makes an ADRT after creating a Health and Welfare LPA, the ADRT takes priority. This means that, even if the attorney has been given authority to make decisions about life-sustaining treatment, they cannot override the ADRT on the issues it covers.

- If the order is reversed, the position changes. Where a donor makes a Health and Welfare LPA after an ADRT and expressly gives the attorney authority to make decisions about life-sustaining treatment, the attorney's decision-making power will override the earlier ADRT to the extent that the two conflict. In simple terms, the law treats the most recent valid expression of the donor's wishes as the one that should be followed.

In practice, problems often arise around whether an ADRT is valid or applies to the situation. The donor must have had capacity when they made it. The ADRT must clearly describe the treatment being refused. If it relates to life-sustaining treatment, it must be in writing, signed and witnessed, and must state clearly that it applies even if the donor's life is at risk. Many ADRTs are written in general terms, which can make it difficult to decide whether they apply to a particular medical situation.

Health and Welfare LPAs can add another layer of complexity. Attorneys and clinicians may disagree about whether an ADRT still applies, especially if it was written many years earlier or before the donor's condition was fully understood. Hospitals may be cautious, particularly where the wording is unclear or family members disagree.

These issues most commonly arise in end-of-life or long-term illness settings. Attorneys may find it distressing to see an ADRT followed where they believe the donor would now choose differently. Clinicians may struggle to interpret instructions that were made long before the donor's health deteriorated. While the legal rules are clear, applying them in real life is often far more difficult.

For this reason, good practice involves careful drafting, regular review of ADRTs, and clear thought about how they are intended to sit alongside a Health and Welfare LPA. Donors should be encouraged to state clearly whether they want an ADRT to continue to apply if they later appoint attorneys, or whether they intend their attorneys to have the final say.

4. Cross-border Authority

Cross-border issues are becoming increasingly important in LPA planning. Many donors now live internationally connected lives. They may own property in more than one country, hold overseas bank accounts or investments, divide their time between jurisdictions or have dual (or multiple) nationality. If such a donor loses capacity, these international links can quickly expose a major weakness in the LPA framework.

LPAs are created under the law of England and Wales. They are designed to work within that legal system and do not automatically have effect outside it. An English LPA does not "travel" with the donor in the way many people assume.

4.1 Will an English LPA be recognised abroad?

Whether an English LPA will be recognised or accepted in another country depends on a complicated and often unpredictable mix of factors. These include local capacity laws, private international law rules and the practical approach taken by banks, land registries and healthcare providers in that jurisdiction.

The Hague Convention on the International Protection of Adults provides a framework for cross-border recognition of protective measures, including powers of attorney. However, the UK's relationship with other Convention states is uneven in practice. Some countries have clear statutory regimes for recognising foreign powers of attorney. Others require formal registration, notarisation or court approval before recognising them. Many jurisdictions make no clear provision at all. As a result, recognition is highly variable and cannot be assumed.

4.2 Practical consequences of non-recognition

The consequences of non-recognition can be serious. Attorneys may find themselves unable to access overseas bank accounts, manage foreign property, or deal with tax obligations at precisely the moment urgent action is needed. Transactions may be delayed or blocked entirely, exposing assets to financial or legal risk.

Difficulties also arise in health and welfare contexts. If a donor loses capacity while abroad, local clinicians may be unfamiliar with the concept of a lasting power of attorney or may be required to follow domestic decision-making frameworks that do not recognise foreign instruments. This can leave attorneys sidelined at critical moments.

These risks mean that cross-border issues should be identified early in the planning process. Where a donor has significant overseas assets or strong links to another jurisdiction, relying solely on an English LPA may be inadequate.

In some cases, the solution is to create a parallel local power of attorney (or equivalent document) in the relevant country, drafted to operate alongside the English LPA. In others, careful structuring of asset ownership, such as holding foreign assets through companies or trusts, may reduce the need for cross-border recognition altogether.

Even where an English LPA ought, in theory, to be recognised abroad, practical obstacles often remain. Foreign banks, investment providers and land registries may impose their own requirements, such as additional identification checks, translations, notarisation or local legal opinions. Tax authorities may require proof of residency or compliance with local reporting rules.

As a result, attorneys may find themselves unable to act in practice, despite having valid authority on paper.

CHAPTER SEVEN

REGISTRATION AND POST-REGISTRATION ISSUES

1. Introduction

The registration of a Lasting Power of Attorney is often perceived as a technical administrative step, something that follows naturally once the donor and attorneys have signed. Yet the registration process performs a constitutional role within the LPA scheme: it is the point at which private delegation of authority becomes a public legal instrument. Registration transforms an LPA from a personal document into one recognised by institutions, courts and public bodies. It is also the moment at which the Office of the OPG fulfils its statutory duty to act as gatekeeper, safeguarding donors against defective LPAs, unlawful clauses, coercion, or mistakes that could compromise their rights.

This chapter explores the registration process, from navigating the OPG's administrative requirements to understanding severance, restrictions and invalid clauses; from managing objections to handling urgent situations when decisions need to be made before registration is complete. These issues carry profound practical significance. They determine whether attorneys can act at the moment of crisis, whether the donor's autonomy is preserved or undermined, and whether the LPA will withstand scrutiny if challenged in the future. Registration is therefore not merely an administrative endpoint to drafting; it is a crucial phase in the lifespan of the LPA.

2. Navigating the OPG Process

The OPG's registration framework is designed to provide accessibility while upholding safeguards. Despite reforms and the increasing use of digital systems, registration remains subject to strict statutory requirements. Any deviation in form, execution or content can lead to delays or rejection.

Registration begins when the donor, or sometimes attorneys, submit the completed LPA to the OPG. Although donors often prefer to register immediately, some choose to delay registration, retaining the LPA in readiness for future use. However, delayed registration carries risks. If a donor loses capacity before registration and a defect is later discovered, it won't be possible to remedy the defect by changing the LPA, leaving deputyship as the only alternative. Early registration reduces the risk of discovering fatal errors too late.

Once an LPA is submitted, the OPG undertakes a review. It checks execution order (donor, certificate provider, attorneys), ensures all signatures are correctly dated, verifies that continuation sheets tally, confirms that attorney details match across the document, and scrutinises instructions and preferences for unlawfulness or inconsistency. Even minor errors such as transposed dates, incorrect placement of a signature, or inconsistent postal addresses can lead to queries or rejection.

The statutory notification process provides a further safeguard. Before registration, certain individuals chosen by the donor must be notified. These persons have the right to object if they believe the LPA is invalid or the donor was pressured. This mechanism creates a transparency and accountability layer before the LPA acquires legal effect.

The OPG's processing times vary. While routine applications may be completed within weeks, more complex cases, particularly those involving severance, objection, or professional attorney involvement, may take significantly longer. More recently, the OPG has been experiencing significant backlogs. For donors approaching mental incapacity, these delays can create anxiety and practical difficulties. Practitioners must therefore anticipate processing time, particularly when LPAs are drafted in the context of emerging cognitive decline or imminent surgery.

Despite the OPG's attempts to modernise, practitioners encounter practical frustrations. Variability in OPG decision-making, inconsistent approaches to borderline clauses, and rigid interpretations of minor drafting choices can create uncertainty. However, such caution reflects the OPG's statutory duty: registration is the final moment at which errors can be remedied without court intervention.

3. Severance, Restrictions and Invalid Clauses

One of the most significant aspects of the OPG's role is the identification of provisions that cannot lawfully stand and must be severed before an LPA can be registered. Severance is not punitive. It is a protective mechanism designed to preserve the validity of the instrument as a whole while ensuring that the statutory scheme governing LPAs is not undermined. Where severance is ordered, the Court of Protection removes the offending provision so far as necessary to give effect to the donor's lawful intentions.

The court's severance jurisdiction must be understood against the wider statutory framework governing the making and registration of LPAs. Schedule 1 to the MCA 2005 sets out mandatory formalities for creating an LPA, including the requirement that the instrument be in the prescribed form and that all prescribed execution requirements are satisfied. If the court determines under section 22(2)(a) MCA 2005 that a requirement for creating the power was not met, it must direct the OPG to cancel the registration.

Severance therefore operates in a distinct space. It is concerned not with whether the instrument was validly executed, but with whether particular terms of an otherwise validly executed LPA are incompatible with the Act. In *The OPG's Severance Applications* [2017] EWCOP 10, District Judge Eldergill explained that severance exists to prevent the statutory safeguards governing attorney authority from being overridden by drafting choices, however well intentioned.

When the OPG identifies clauses in an LPA that either purport to confer powers that exceed statutory limits or otherwise invalidate the instrument, it refers the matter to the Court of Protection. The court then determines whether the offending provision can be severed or whether the defect is so fundamental that registration must be refused. In practice, the court generally seeks to preserve the instrument by severance, reflecting the strong statutory preference for giving effect to a donor's intention where possible.

However, severance can materially alter the operation of an LPA. Clauses drafted as binding instructions may disappear entirely from the registered document. Attorneys should be advised that severance reflects legal necessity rather than donor preference, and that they remain bound by the MCA's best-interests framework, not by excised provisions.

Complex or internally inconsistent appointment structures present particular difficulties. Where donors attempt to create hybrid arrangements that are unclear or contradictory, the court may sever those provisions and default to a simpler joint and several appointment. While this preserves functionality, it may dilute a donor's nuanced intentions.

It is important to distinguish severance from the court's separate power to cure defects in form. Paragraph 3(2) of Schedule 1 MCA 2005 permits the court to declare that an instrument not in the prescribed form is to be treated as if it were, provided the court is satisfied that those executing it intended to create an LPA. This "dispensing power" traces back to the Law Commission's concern that donors should not be defeated by technical or "pettifogging" defects where intention is clear. The court has used this power to remedy a range of execution defects, including missing confirmations, failures to date the instrument, or minor errors in names and addresses.

The limits of this power are, however, well established. It cannot rescue an instrument that has not been adequately executed at all. As Senior Judge Lush observed in *Re Lodge* (unreported), and as reaffirmed by District Judge Eldergill in The OPG's Severance Applications, paragraph 3(2) cannot cure execution in the wrong order or situations where the donor and attorneys have executed the wrong parts of the form. These are not defects of form but failures to create the power.

The distinction between severable defects and fatal invalidity was illustrated again in *Re OPGs Severance Applications* [2023] EWCOP 24. The case underscores that while the court is willing to be flexible where donor intention is clear, it will not stretch either the severance jurisdiction or the dispensing power beyond their statutory limits. Where fundamental requirements for creating an LPA are not met, the instrument cannot be salvaged by judicial ingenuity.

Best practice therefore demands clarity, restraint and a close understanding of the statutory boundaries. The more an LPA seeks to dictate outcomes or to depart from the statutory framework, the greater the risk of intervention by the OPG or the court. Careful drafting remains the most effective safeguard against severance and invalidity alike.

4. Objections to Registration

Objections to the registration of an LPA may be raised either on factual grounds, such as concerns about donor capacity, fraud or undue influence, or on prescribed grounds under the regulations. An objection does not automatically halt registration, but it triggers a more formal process requiring investigation.

Objections can come from two sources: notified persons (usually relatives or close friends) or attorneys themselves. Notifications play a crucial role: they allow those closest to the donor to scrutinise the circumstances of execution. Notified persons may object if they believe the donor lacked capacity, if someone exerted undue influence, or if an attorney is unsuitable due to personal conduct, bankruptcy or conflict of interest.

When an objection is raised, the OPG must evaluate its merits. In some cases, the OPG can resolve factual questions administratively: confirming identity, checking dates or clarifying minor misunderstandings. In others, the objection triggers referral to the Court of Protection. The court may require evidence of capacity, testimony from the certificate provider or statements from attorneys and family members. In complex or highly contested cases, medical and safeguarding evidence may be necessary.

Objections can have long-lasting family consequences. Accusations of undue influence, in particular, can fracture relationships. Practitioners advising donors should therefore explore family dynamics before drafting LPAs, anticipating whether notifications may prompt conflict.

Objections also arise when attorneys themselves dispute aspects of the LPA. Sometimes attorneys disagree about their roles; sometimes they contest preferences or instructions. The court must then determine whether the donor's intention was clear and whether registration should proceed.

Ultimately, the objection process serves as a safeguard, ensuring that LPAs reflect genuine, voluntary decisions. While objections can be disruptive and emotionally fraught, they prevent harmful LPAs from entering operation.

5. Interim Decision-Making and Urgent Situations

A significant practical challenge arises when urgent decisions are required before an LPA is registered. Attorneys have no authority to act until registration is complete, no matter how pressing the donor's circumstances. This creates a tension between the donor's need for immediate support and the legal requirement for prior registration.

Urgent situations are most common in financial contexts. Bills may need to be paid, care home fees demanded, or property transactions requiring signatures may be underway. If the donor has lost capacity and the LPA is still in registration, delays can cause financial instability or missed opportunities. Banks, solicitors and institutions generally refuse to recognise unregistered LPAs, and attorneys have no legal basis to compel cooperation.

In welfare contexts, urgent decisions may arise about care arrangements, hospital discharges or medical treatment. However, because a Health and Welfare LPA cannot be used until the donor lacks capacity, some of these decisions may fall within the professionals' best interests duties rather than the attorneys'. Even so, attorneys waiting for registration may feel excluded from processes they expect to control.

The Court of Protection can provide interim relief through urgent or emergency applications. In financial emergencies, the court may authorise attorneys to make specific decisions pending registration. In welfare contexts, the court may clarify authority or determine best interests. However, these applications can be costly, stressful and time-sensitive. The need for court intervention underscores the importance of early registration and thorough planning.

Practitioners should warn donors of these risks. Donors who delay registration often assume they can register the LPA later when needed, not realising that incapacity may strike before registration is possible. Early registration avoids these liminal periods where no one has legal authority to act.

In emergencies, the court can appoint an interim deputy. This may undermine the donor's anticipatory planning, but it provides necessary governance in critical moments. In such cases, once the LPA is registered, the deputyship may be discharged or limited to avoid duplication.

CHAPTER EIGHT

REVOCATION, SUSPENSION AND TERMINATION

1. Introduction

Revocation and termination intersect with some of the most sensitive moments in the LPA's lifespan: the donor's fluctuating capacity, safeguarding concerns, breakdowns in trust, the deterioration or misconduct of attorneys and the involvement of the Court of Protection. These issues often arise at times of crisis, when the donor's personal circumstances are fragile or complex. For attorneys, recognising the boundaries of their authority and knowing when it ends is fundamental to maintaining fiduciary integrity. For professionals, understanding the legal mechanisms of revocation and termination helps prevent inadvertent breaches of authority. For courts and the OPG, these mechanisms serve as essential safeguards.

This chapter explores revocation by the donor, the effect of loss and restoration of capacity, the automatic termination events set by statute, the Court of Protection's role in modifying or ending an LPA, and the process for removing or replacing attorneys. Across these themes, the law balances the donor's autonomy with the need to protect them from detriment.

2. Donor Revocation

The donor retains the right to revoke an LPA at any time while they have capacity to do so. This reflects a fundamental principle of autonomy: the same capacity required to create an LPA is required to revoke it. The donor must understand the nature and effect of revocation, including the consequence that attorneys will no longer have authority to act. They need not articulate detailed reasons, but they must demonstrate that the decision is knowing, voluntary and informed.

Revocation may arise for many reasons. Donors may lose trust in an attorney, especially if family dynamics deteriorate. They may reconcile with estranged relatives or form new relationships, prompting a change in who they wish to appoint. Donors may also revoke in circumstances where their life circumstances have shifted significantly, having moved home, remarried or simplified their finances.

The capacity threshold mirrors that for making the LPA itself, but revocation carries a particular complexity. Donors experiencing early cognitive decline may retain capacity for some decisions but struggle with complex matters; they may express fluctuating views about attorneys, influenced by emotional instability or family conflict. Professionals must ensure that revocation does not arise from coercion, fear, misunderstanding or delusion. The certificate provider's protections no longer apply at the point of revocation, so practitioners play an essential safeguarding role.

A donor with capacity may also revoke the appointment of one attorney while preserving the rest, provided the LPA permits this. Where attorneys are appointed jointly, revocation of one attorney may invalidate the entire appointment structure. Donors must understand that revoking one attorney in a joint arrangement may collapse the whole mechanism. Revocation is therefore not merely a private expression of preference; it reshapes the legal structure governing future decision-making.

3. Court of Protection Revocation

The Court of Protection is the ultimate arbiter of the validity, interpretation, operation and termination of lasting powers of attorney. While LPAs are intended to allow decision-making to take place without routine court involvement, the MCA 2005 establishes a clear supervisory jurisdiction to ensure that attorneys act lawfully and that donors are protected from abuse, exploitation or neglect.

The court's jurisdiction extends to determining whether an LPA has been validly made, resolving disputes about its meaning or scope, directing attorneys as to how they should exercise their powers, suspending or terminating attorney appointments, and, where necessary, appointing deputies to replace attorneys. These powers are grounded primarily in sections 22 and 23 MCA 2005 and are reinforced by the MCA Code of Practice, which emphasises that court intervention is a safeguard of last resort rather than a routine feature of LPA operation.

Court involvement may arise in a variety of ways: following an investigation by the Office of the OPG; through applications brought by family members or co-attorneys; as a result of concerns raised by professionals such as banks, care providers or solicitors; or through safeguarding referrals from local authorities. In each case, the court's task is to balance respect for the donor's autonomy with the need to protect them from harm.

The court's power to revoke an LPA arises under section 22(4) MCA 2005. The circumstances in which that power may be exercised are set out in section 22(3). In summary, the court may revoke an LPA if it is satisfied that the attorney (or any one of multiple attorneys):

- has behaved, or is behaving, in a way that contravenes their authority or is not in the donor's best interests; or

- proposes to behave in a way that would contravene their authority or would not be in the donor's best interests.

This formulation is deliberately broad. It allows the court to intervene not only where misconduct has already occurred, but also where there is a real risk of future harm. The focus is protective rather than punitive, and the court is concerned with the effect of the attorney's conduct on the donor, rather than the attorney's motives.

Case law illustrates that revocation may be justified by a wide range of behaviours. Clear examples include financial abuse, unauthorised gifts, misuse or mixing of funds, failure to keep accounts, or using the donor's assets for personal benefit. Revocation may also be appropriate where attorneys repeatedly fail to consult the donor, ignore their known wishes and values, or act in ways that are plainly incompatible with the donor's best interests as defined by section 4 MCA 2005.

Importantly, revocation is not limited to cases of dishonesty or bad faith. Attorneys who are well-intentioned but incompetent, conflicted or unable to work constructively with others may also be removed if their conduct places the donor at risk. Persistent failure to engage with professionals, refusal to provide information to the OPG, or an inability to make necessary decisions can all ground revocation.

The MCA Code of Practice reinforces this approach. It emphasises that attorneys must act within the scope of their authority, must always act in the donor's best interests, and must be able to explain and justify their decisions. Where these duties are breached, court intervention may be required.

Section 22(3) expressly permits revocation where an attorney proposes to behave in a way that would contravene their authority or the donor's best interests. This forward-looking element is significant. It enables the court to intervene before irreversible harm occurs, for example where an attorney indicates an intention to sell property without proper justification, make substantial gifts without authority, or exclude the donor from decision-making altogether.

In such cases, the court will carefully assess whether the proposed conduct genuinely presents a risk, and whether lesser measures, such as directions or temporary suspension, would be sufficient. Revocation remains a measure of last resort.

3.1 Revocation procedure

Applications to revoke an LPA are fact-sensitive and procedurally demanding. Because revocation interferes directly with the donor's autonomy and with the donor's prior choice of attorney, the Court of Protection approaches such applications with particular care. The court's task is not to resolve family disputes or to determine what it would have done differently, but to decide whether the statutory threshold in section 22(3) MCA 2005 is met.

Applications to revoke an LPA most commonly arise following an investigation by the Office of the OPG. Concerns may be raised by relatives, care providers, banks, solicitors or local authorities, prompting the OPG to exercise its investigatory powers. If those investigations suggest that an attorney has acted, or proposes to act, outside their authority or contrary to the donor's best interests, the OPG may apply to the Court of Protection for revocation.

Revocation applications may also be brought by co-attorneys, family members or other interested parties. In high-conflict cases, the donor (through a litigation friend) may be a party. The court retains control of proceedings and will often case-manage actively from an early stage.

Evidence required

The court will typically expect a detailed evidential foundation demonstrating why the statutory test is met. Depending on the nature of the allegations, evidence may include:

- Financial evidence, such as bank statements, accounts, records of transfers or gifts, and explanations for expenditure;

- Witness statements from family members, carers, professionals or safeguarding teams describing concerns about behaviour, decision-making or neglect;

- Medical or capacity evidence, particularly where revocation is linked to decisions made at a time when capacity was borderline or fluctuating;

- Evidence from the attorney, including explanations of decisions, accounting records, and statements addressing the allegations;

- OPG investigation reports, which often play a central role in framing the issues.

The standard of proof is the civil standard, namely the balance of probabilities. However, as the case law makes clear, the seriousness of the allegations and the gravity of the consequences require careful and rigorous evaluation of the evidence. In *The OPG v AC* [2014] EWCOP 41, for example, the court emphasised the importance of clear financial evidence demonstrating misuse of funds, rather than generalised assertions of concern. Unsupported suspicion or family dissatisfaction is rarely sufficient.

3.2 Types of hearings

Applications to revoke a lasting power of attorney can involve a range of hearings, reflecting both the complexity of the issues and the Court of Protection's flexible, problem-solving approach. While some cases resolve quickly, others progress through several procedural stages before final determination. Understanding the different types of hearings that may arise is essential for effective case preparation and proportionate litigation.

Proceedings are governed by the Court of Protection Rules 2017, which emphasise flexibility, active case management and the overriding objective of dealing with cases justly, proportionately and with proper regard to the vulnerability of those involved. In LPA revocation cases, the court is often required to balance urgency, safeguarding concerns and contested evidence.

Dispute Resolution Hearing (DRH)

In property and affairs cases, and increasingly in LPA revocation proceedings, the court will often list an initial Dispute Resolution Hearing. This has become close to standard practice in contested financial applications.

At a DRH, the judge adopts a quasi-inquisitorial and facilitative role. The hearing is usually relatively informal. The judge will explore the issues in dispute, test the parties' positions, and may give a provisional or evaluative view of the likely outcome if the matter proceeds to a final hearing. The purpose is not to determine the case, but to encourage realistic appraisal and early resolution.

In LPA revocation cases, a DRH may expose whether concerns could be addressed through directions, undertakings, accounting exercises or limited restrictions on attorney powers, rather than full revocation. Many cases settle or narrow significantly at this stage.

Urgent and interim hearings

Urgent hearings may be listed where there is an immediate risk to the donor's welfare or property, such as suspected financial abuse, threatened asset dissipation, or serious safeguarding concerns. In such cases, the court may be willing to exercise its interim jurisdiction under section 48 MCA 2005, even where full evidence of lack of capacity is not yet available.

At an urgent hearing, the court may make interim protective orders, including suspending an attorney's powers, restricting transactions or requiring urgent disclosure of financial information. These hearings are often conducted on limited notice and based on incomplete evidence, reflecting the protective nature of the court's jurisdiction.

Interim orders are not determinative of the final outcome. Their function is to stabilise the situation pending fuller investigation and evidence.

Round table meetings

Round table meetings are a distinctive feature of Court of Protection practice and are frequently used in LPA disputes. They are typically meetings between the parties and their representatives, and may sometimes include other professionals involved in the donor's life, such as social workers or care providers.

The purpose of a round table meeting is to narrow the issues in dispute, clarify areas of agreement, and identify what genuinely requires judicial determination. In revocation cases, this may involve agreeing factual matters, identifying which transactions or decisions are disputed, or determining whether alternative protective measures could avoid revocation.

Round table meetings can be particularly valuable where family conflict risks overwhelming the substantive issues. They help ensure that the court's time is focused on matters that truly affect the donor's protection.

Directions hearings

Directions hearings are used to case-manage proceedings and to ensure that evidence is obtained efficiently and proportionately. At these hearings, the court may give directions for disclosure, accounting exercises, expert evidence, witness statements or OPG investigations.

In revocation cases, directions hearings are often critical in shaping the litigation. The court may decide whether a fact-finding hearing is necessary, whether issues can be resolved on the papers, or whether a more evaluative approach is appropriate. The court will also consider whether interim safeguards should remain in place.

Directions hearings are usually relatively short but play a decisive role in controlling the scope and cost of proceedings.

Fact-finding

Where material facts are disputed, the court may list a fact-finding hearing. This is particularly common where allegations of financial abuse, coercion or neglect are denied by the attorney. Fact-finding hearings may involve oral evidence, cross-examination of witnesses, and close scrutiny of documentary records.

Fact-finding hearings can be emotionally charged, time-consuming and costly, both financially and in human terms. For that reason, the Court of Protection will often consider whether concerns can be addressed through narrower procedural steps, such as focused disclosure, directions for accounts, interim restrictions on attorney powers, or OPG supervision, before embarking on a full evidential hearing involving oral evidence and cross-examination.

There is also a more fundamental question as to whether fact-finding hearings are always an effective or appropriate mechanism in LPA revocation cases, particularly where the concern is not a single discrete act of misconduct but an alleged pattern of behaviour over time. Many revocation applications are not founded on one provable transaction or decision, but on an accumulation of conduct: repeated failures to consult, consistent disregard for the donor's wishes, or an entrenched conflict of interest. Such cases raise difficulties for traditional fact-finding methodologies.

The court's experience in the family jurisdiction offers a helpful analogy. In that context, the appellate courts have repeatedly cautioned against unnecessary or over-elaborate fact-finding exercises where the issue is not whether a specific incident occurred, but whether there is a broader pattern of behaviour relevant to welfare decisions. In *Re H-N and Others (Children)* [2021] EWCA Civ 448, the Court of Appeal observed that domestic abuse often manifests as a pattern of coercive or controlling behaviour rather than as isolated incidents capable of binary proof. The court warned that an excessive focus on individual allegations, itemised in schedules, may obscure the true nature of the risk and divert attention from the evaluative task the court is required to undertake.

Similar concerns arise in the Court of Protection. The use of Scott Schedules, for example, may assist in identifying specific disputed transactions or events, but they are poorly suited to capturing systemic issues such as ongoing neglect of duties, misuse of discretion or an attorney's consistent prioritisation of their own interests. Proving or disproving individual entries in a schedule may do little to illuminate whether the attorney's overall conduct is incompatible with the statutory duties imposed by the MCA 2005.

3.2 Interim protective measures

Where concerns arise but the evidence is incomplete or still under investigation, the court may order the suspension of an attorney's powers or impose interim restrictions. These interim measures are a critical part of the court's toolkit. They allow the donor's interests to be protected without prematurely terminating the LPA or undermining the donor's original choice of attorney.

Interim orders may include suspending an attorney's authority pending further evidence, prohibiting specific transactions, limiting access to funds, or requiring attorneys to provide accounts or explanations of past decisions. The Code of Practice recognises the importance of proportionate responses and supports the use of temporary safeguards where appropriate. Such orders reflect the court's preference for incremental intervention rather than immediate removal.

4. What happens after an LPA is revoked?

Revocation of an LPA does not leave a vacuum. Once the court has determined that an attorney should be removed and that the LPA can no longer safely operate, it must decide how the donor's affairs are to be managed going forward. The court's focus immediately shifts from retrospective scrutiny of the attorney's conduct to prospective protection of the donor's welfare and property.

The consequences of revocation depend first on the structure of the LPA itself. Where the donor has named replacement attorneys, those individuals may step into the role automatically upon revocation of the original attorney's appointment. Similarly, where multiple attorneys were appointed jointly and severally, and only one is removed, the LPA may continue to operate through the remaining attorneys. In such cases, further court involvement may be limited, although the court may still impose directions or safeguards if concerns remain.

However, where the removal of an attorney causes the appointment structure to fail, for example, where attorneys were appointed jointly and one is removed, or where all attorneys are removed, the LPA can no longer function. In those circumstances, the court must determine how decisions are to be made on the donor's behalf.

The statutory mechanism for filling that gap is found in section 16(2) of the MCA 2005. Under that provision, the court may either make specific decisions itself on the donor's behalf, or appoint a deputy to make decisions on an ongoing basis. In practice, where an LPA has been revoked and ongoing decision-making is required, the court will usually appoint a deputy.

The appointment of a deputy is not automatic, and the court will consider whether deputyship is necessary and proportionate in light of the donor's needs, for example, if the donor has limited funds, the court is unlikely to appoint a deputy just because they previously had an attorney. However, where the donor lacks capacity in the relevant domain and there is no functioning LPA, deputyship is often the only practical means of ensuring continuity of decision-making and financial management.

In *Re Lawson, Mottram and Hopton* [2019] EWCOP 22, the court emphasised that the appointment of a personal welfare deputy is exceptional and must be justified by the particular circumstances of the case.

The choice of deputy is a matter of considerable importance. The court will assess who is best placed to act in the donor's best interests, taking into account the nature of the decisions required, the history of the case, and the level of conflict or complexity involved.

In cases following the revocation of an LPA, the court often favours the appointment of a professional deputy, particularly where family conflict has contributed to the breakdown of the LPA. Professional deputies are seen as offering neutrality, expertise and stability and their appointment may reduce the risk of further disputes. However, this comes at a financial cost to the donor's estate and may alter family dynamics significantly.

Where a family member seeks appointment as deputy, the court will scrutinise their suitability carefully, particularly if they were involved in the events leading to revocation. Prior misconduct does not automatically preclude appointment, but unresolved concerns or entrenched conflict may weigh heavily against it.

CHAPTER NINE

FUTURE DEVELOPMENTS AND REFORM

1. Introduction

Lasting Powers of Attorney, though rooted in the MCA 2005, are instruments that sit at the crossroads of law, policy, technology and social change. Their evolution will be shaped not only by legislative reform but by broader cultural expectations about autonomy, ageing, digital identity and cross-border mobility. As populations live longer, family structures diversify, global travel becomes commonplace and technology transforms the way individuals verify themselves and manage their finances, the LPA system must adapt. The future of LPAs is therefore not simply a question of statutory amendment but of reimagining how society empowers individuals to plan for incapacity within a rapidly shifting landscape.

This chapter explores the forces driving reform: the government's digital LPA modernisation programme; the role of technological change, digital identity systems and algorithmic verification; debates about safeguarding, attorney oversight and state involvement; and the emerging international convergence in adult incapacity law. LPAs, once conceived as paper forms signed at a kitchen table, are becoming sophisticated legal instruments that must integrate with digital governance and global financial systems. The challenge for reform is to balance accessibility with protection, efficiency with rigour, and personal autonomy with robust safeguards.

The future trajectory of LPAs will reflect tensions between competing values. Increasing technological automation promises smoother registration but raises concerns about fraud. Enhanced oversight offers greater protection but risks paternalism or bureaucratic burden. International recognition supports global mobility but complicates domestic jurisdiction. These tensions are not merely theoretical; they shape the lived experience of donors and attorneys. A reformed LPA system must therefore speak to the realities of 21st-century life while remaining faithful to the fundamental principles of the MCA 2005.

2. Digital LPAs

2.1 The Government's Modernisation Programme

The most significant current reform initiative is the move towards digital LPAs, introduced by the Powers of Attorney Act 2023. The Act provides the statutory framework for a new, digital-first system for creating and registering LPAs, overseen by the Ministry of Justice and the Office of the Public Guardian. Its aim is to move away from a wholly paper-based process towards a secure digital ecosystem. It is due to begin implementation in 2026.

The reform responds to a number of well-recognised pressures: the steadily increasing volume of LPAs, persistent delays in registration, and concerns about fraud, coercion and defective execution. By redesigning the process rather than simply digitising paper forms, the legislation seeks to modernise both access to LPAs and the safeguards surrounding them.

Digital LPAs promise several practical benefits. They should enable faster processing and significantly reduce registration delays, which currently can run to many weeks or months. A structured digital system can prevent common execution errors, such as missing signatures, incorrect dates or incomplete forms, by embedding checks directly into the process. Automated notifications can ensure that relevant parties are informed at the appropriate stages, reducing disputes based on lack of notice. Digital storage also removes the ongoing risk of lost or damaged original documents, a problem that frequently arises years after an LPA has been made.

Yet digitisation is not simply administrative convenience; it represents a philosophical shift. LPAs have historically relied on physical presence and handwritten signatures as markers of authenticity and voluntariness. A digital system must replicate these protective functions in new ways. The modernisation programme envisages the use of secure government-backed identity checks, multi-factor authentication and verification through GOV.UK systems. These measures could reduce impersonation risks but require public trust in digital governance.

A digital certificate provider process presents particular safeguarding challenges. The certificate provider must still be able to speak to the donor privately, without attorneys or family members present, to assess whether the decision is voluntary. In a digital setting, this may require video meetings, secure messaging or other verification methods to confirm the certificate provider's independence. There remains a question as to whether digital processes can reliably replicate the informal but important cues that help identify pressure or undue influence in face-to-face meetings.

Digital execution also raises questions about inclusivity. Not all donors, especially older individuals or those with fluctuating capacity, are comfortable with digital systems. The government has pledged to retain a paper-route alternative, but parallel systems risk complexity and duplication of effort. Ensuring equal access across socio-economic and generational groups is therefore essential to avoid excluding those whom the system is meant to protect.

Ultimately, the digital modernisation programme illustrates the tension between efficiency and safeguarding. If successful, it could transform LPAs into more robust and accessible instruments. But if implemented without sufficient attention to vulnerability, it could increase the risk of exploitation.

2.2 Technological Change and Identity Verification

Artificial intelligence may also play a role in screening LPAs for internal inconsistencies or detecting markers of undue influence. Machine learning systems trained on historical OPG cases could flag risk patterns. However, automated decision-making introduces significant ethical concerns. Algorithms may reproduce bias or misinterpret cultural or linguistic differences. A future LPA system must therefore integrate AI tools carefully, ensuring human oversight remains central.

The medical context also drives innovation. As healthcare records become digital, attorneys may be granted structured digital access to the donor's medical profile. This raises questions about confidentiality, data minimisation and the boundaries of attorney authority. Clear statutory guidance will be required to prevent misuse or overreach.

Technological change therefore has a dual nature: it promises stronger safeguards, yet creates new vulnerabilities. Law reform must anticipate these developments to ensure LPAs remain effective and trustworthy.

3. Proposals for further reform

The balance between autonomy and protection is an enduring theme in capacity law, and it remains central to debates about LPA reform. Increasing case law and OPG investigations reveal persistent challenges: financial abuse by attorneys, conflicts of interest, absence of record-keeping, and failure to apply the best interests test. These concerns fuel arguments for stronger oversight.

Ideas for reform vary widely:

1. Some suggest that attorneys should be required to complete basic training before an LPA can be used, so they clearly understand their responsibilities from the outset. This could take the form of

simple online guidance or short interactive courses, helping to prevent mistakes made through lack of awareness.

2. Others propose closer oversight once an LPA is in use, particularly where large sums of money are involved. This might include periodic reporting, such as annual financial summaries or occasional spot checks. The aim would be to discourage misuse and make decision-making more transparent, without turning LPAs into an overly burdensome system. However, increased oversight carries significant resource implications for the OPG and may impose burdens on families. Critics warn that excessive monitoring risks transforming LPAs into quasi-deputyship arrangements, undermining the donor's autonomy and the system's accessibility. The challenge is to design proportional safeguards that target risk without stifling autonomy.

3. A related debate concerns certificate providers. Some argue for introducing professional qualification requirements, ensuring providers possess competency in assessing voluntariness and capacity. Others support expanding the role to include structured screening tools or enhanced documentation. Conversely, critics caution against restricting the pool of certificate providers, fearing increased cost and reduced accessibility for donors without professional networks.

4. Finally, debates centre on attorney selection. Some practitioners suggest allowing donors to appoint supervisory attorneys who oversee or audit other attorneys' decisions. Others propose requiring donors who appoint only one attorney to provide justification or appoint a replacement. These approaches may reduce the risk of concentrated authority but must be weighed against donor freedom to structure their affairs as they choose.

The future of LPAs will depend on how these debates are resolved. The system must evolve to address vulnerabilities without undermining the core principle that donors, not the state, choose their decision-makers.

4. International Trends and the Role of LPAs in a Globalised World

LPAs are increasingly part of a global movement toward supported decision-making and advanced planning for incapacity. Many jurisdictions now recognise or are developing equivalent instruments. Comparative analysis reveals converging trends: rising cross-border mobility, growing concerns about elder financial abuse and increased reliance on digital governance.

One major international development is the Hague Convention on the International Protection of Adults. Although the UK participates selectively, the Convention creates a framework for recognising foreign powers of attorney and coordinating authority across borders. As more countries adopt the Convention, LPAs may gain greater international portability. Yet significant hurdles remain: conflict-of-laws questions, divergent capacity standards, and inconsistent local recognition procedures all impede seamless operation. Reformers argue for greater UK engagement with international frameworks to facilitate recognition of LPAs abroad and acceptance of foreign equivalents in the UK.

Another trend is the shift toward supported decision-making models following the influence of the UN Convention on the Rights of Persons with Disabilities. Some jurisdictions are experimenting with legally recognised "supporters" rather than substitute decision-makers. While the MCA 2005 incorporates support principles, LPAs remain fundamentally substitutive mechanisms. Future reform may involve hybrid models that integrate supported decision-making more explicitly, requiring attorneys to document how they enabled the donor's participation even when the donor lacks capacity.

Globalisation also influences financial and business aspects of LPAs. Donors with foreign property, international investments or cross-border business interests require LPAs that operate effectively across jurisdictions. Reform may involve clearer statutory provisions on choice of law, recognition of foreign decision-making instruments, or the creation of international LPA certification systems similar to apostilles for notarised documents.

In sum, LPAs are increasingly part of a global conversation about autonomy, ageing and protection. The UK's future reform should be informed by, and contribute to, this international evolution.

5. Conclusion

This book has looked at Lasting Powers of Attorney as more than legal paperwork. LPAs sit at the meeting point of personal choice, vulnerability, trust and safeguarding. By exploring how they developed, how they are used in practice and how they operate across finances, health and welfare, business and complex estates, the book shows what LPAs look like in real life.

The focus throughout has been on practical decision-making: understanding when LPAs work well, where problems tend to arise and how careful drafting, sensible choice of attorneys and a clear grasp of capacity and best interests can help prevent disputes and harm. As the system continues to change, particularly with the move towards digital LPAs, the core challenge remains the same: how to respect a person's independence while making sure they are properly protected if they lose capacity.

LPAs are not simply documents to be signed and put away. They are ongoing arrangements that require thought, care and professional responsibility from start to finish.

MORE BOOKS BY LAW BRIEF PUBLISHING

A selection of our other titles available now:-

'A Practical Guide to Probation Breaches and Other Applications' by Mark Thomas
'A Practical Guide to Remarriage and Divorce' by Cordelia Williams & Claire Howard
'A Practical Guide to Privacy, Transparency, Reporting Restrictions and Closed Proceedings in the Court of Protection' by Laura Mannering
'Beaumont on Barristers – A Guide to Defending Disciplinary Proceedings (Second Edition)' by Marc Beaumont
'A Practical Guide to Payments for Environmental Services' by Ben Sharples
'A Practical Guide to the Law of Pregnancy and Maternity at Work' by Rebecca Thomas
'A Practical Guide to Redundancy – Second Edition' by Philip Hyland & Collette Moore
'A Practical Guide to International Issues for Scottish Family Lawyers' by Susie Mountain, Donna McKay, Ken MacDonald
'A Practical Guide to the Law on Deprivation of Liberty' by Ben Troke
'A Practical Guide to Rights over Airspace and Subsoil – Second Edition' by Daniel Gatty
'A Practical Guide to the Law in Relation to Inquests' by Ramya Nagesh
'A Practical Guide to the Construction and Rectification of Wills and Trust Instruments (Second Edition)' by Edward Hewitt
'A Practical Guide to Data Protection in Social Housing' by Clare Paterson
'A Practical Guide to Spousal Maintenance – Second Edition' by Liz Cowell
'A Practical Guide to International Parental Child Abduction Law (England and Wales)' by Dr Onyója Momoh
'A Practical Guide to Deprivation of British Citizenship' by Sean Ell
'A Practical Guide to Commercial Property Service Charges' by Rachel Garton
'A Practical Guide to Clinical Negligence – Third Edition' by Geoffrey Simpson-Scott (Geoff)
'A Practical Guide to the Rights of Grandparents in Children Proceedings – Second Edition' by Stuart Barlow

'The Electronic Communications Code: A Practical Guide – Second Edition' by Kerry Bretherton KC, James Castle, Mark Loveday
'A Practical Guide to the Independent School Standards – September 2023 Edition' by Sarah McKimm
'A Practical Guide to Estate Administration and Crypto Assets' by Richard Marshall
'A Practical Guide to Parental Alienation in Private and Public Law Children Cases' by Sam King QC & Frankie Shama
'Contested Heritage – Removing Art from Land and Historic Buildings' by Richard Harwood QC, Catherine Dobson, David Sawtell
'The Limits of Separate Legal Personality: When Those Running a Company Can Be Held Personally Liable for Losses Caused to Third Parties Outside of the Company' by Dr Mike Wilkinson
'A Practical Guide to Transgender Law' by Robin Moira White & Nicola Newbegin
'A Practical Guide to 'Stranded Spouses' in Family Law' by Mani Singh Basi
'A Practical Guide to Residential Freehold Conveyancing' by Lorraine Richardson
'A Practical Guide to Pensions on Divorce for Lawyers' by Bryan Scant
'A Practical Guide to Challenging Sham Marriage Allegations in Immigration Law' by Priya Solanki
'A Practical Guide to Digital Communications Evidence in Criminal Law' by Sam Willis
'A Practical Guide to Legal Rights in Scotland' by Sarah-Jane Macdonald
'A Practical Guide to New Build Conveyancing' by Paul Sams & Rebecca East
'A Practical Guide to Inherited Wealth on Divorce' by Hayley Trim
'A Practical Guide to Practice Direction 12J and Domestic Abuse in Private Law Children Proceedings' by Rebecca Cross & Malvika Jaganmohan
'A Practical Guide to Confiscation and Restraint' by Narita Bahra QC, John Carl Townsend, David Winch
'A Practical Guide to the Law of Forests in Scotland' by Philip Buchan
'A Practical Guide to Health and Medical Cases in Immigration Law' by Rebecca Chapman & Miranda Butler
'A Practical Guide to Bad Character Evidence for Criminal Practitioners by Aparna Rao
'A Practical Guide to Extradition Law post-Brexit' by Myles Grandison et al
'A Practical Guide to Hoarding and Mental Health for Housing Lawyers' by Rachel Coyle

'Stephens on Contractual Indemnities' by Richard Stephens

'A Practical Guide to the EU Succession Regulation' by Richard Frimston

'A Practical Guide to Solicitor and Client Costs – Second Edition' by Robin Dunne

'Constructive Dismissal – Practice Pointers and Principles' by Benjimin Burgher

'A Practical Guide to Religion and Belief Discrimination Claims in the Workplace' by Kashif Ali

'A Practical Guide to the Law of Medical Treatment Decisions' by Ben Troke

'Fundamental Dishonesty and QOCS in Personal Injury Proceedings: Law and Practice' by Jake Rowley

'A Practical Guide to the Law in Relation to School Exclusions' by Charlotte Hadfield & Alice de Coverley

'A Practical Guide to Divorce for the Silver Separators' by Karin Walker

'The Right to be Forgotten – The Law and Practical Issues' by Melissa Stock

'A Practical Guide to Planning Law and Rights of Way in National Parks, the Broads and AONBs' by James Maurici QC, James Neill et al

'A Practical Guide to Election Law' by Tom Tabori

'A Practical Guide to the Law in Relation to Surrogacy' by Andrew Powell

'A Practical Guide to Claims Arising from Fatal Accidents – Second Edition' by James Patience

'A Practical Guide to Asbestos Claims' by Jonathan Owen & Gareth McAloon

'A Practical Guide to Stamp Duty Land Tax in England and Northern Ireland' by Suzanne O'Hara

'A Practical Guide to the Law of Farming Partnerships' by Philip Whitcomb

'A Practical Guide to the Law of Unlawful Eviction and Harassment – Second Edition' by Stephanie Lovegrove

'A Practical Guide to Costs in Personal Injury Claims – Second Edition' by Matthew Hoe

'A Practical Guide to the General Data Protection Regulation (GDPR) – Second Edition' by Keith Markham

'A Practical Guide to Working with Litigants in Person and McKenzie Friends in Family Cases' by Stuart Barlow

'Protecting Unregistered Brands: A Practical Guide to the Law of Passing Off' by Lorna Brazell

'A Practical Guide to Secondary Liability and Joint Enterprise Post-Jogee' by Joanne Cecil & James Mehigan

'A Practical Guide to the Pre-Action RTA Claims Protocol for Personal Injury Lawyers' by Antonia Ford

'A Practical Guide to Neighbour Disputes and the Law' by Alexander Walsh

'A Practical Guide to Coercive Control for Legal Practitioners and Victims' by Rachel Horman

'A Practical Guide to the Law of Driverless Cars – Second Edition'

by Alex Glassbrook, Emma Northey & Scarlett Milligan

'A Practical Guide to TOLATA Claims' by Greg Williams

'A Practical Guide to Elderly Law – Second Edition' by Justin Patten

'A Practical Guide to Responding to Housing Disrepair and Unfitness Claims' by Iain Wightwick

'A Practical Guide to the Law of Bullying and Harassment in the Workplace' by Philip Hyland

'How to Be a Freelance Solicitor: A Practical Guide to the SRA-Regulated Freelance Solicitor Model' by Paul Bennett

'A Practical Guide to Prison Injury Claims' by Malcolm Johnson

'A Practical Guide to Advising Clients at the Police Station' by Colin Stephen McKeown-Beaumont

'A Practical Guide to Antisocial Behaviour Injunctions – Second Edition' by Iain Wightwick

'Practical Mediation: A Guide for Mediators, Advocates, Advisers, Lawyers, and Students in Civil, Commercial, Business, Property, Workplace, and Employment Cases' by Jonathan Dingle with John Sephton

'The Mini-Pupillage Workbook' by David Boyle

'A Practical Guide to Crofting Law' by Brian Inkster

'A Practical Guide to the Law of Domain Names and Cybersquatting' by Andrew Clemson

'A Practical Guide to the Law of Gender Pay Gap Reporting' by Harini Iyengar

'NHS Whistleblowing and the Law' by Joseph England

'Employment Law and the Gig Economy' by Nigel Mackay & Annie Powell

'A Practical Guide to Noise Induced Hearing Loss (NIHL) Claims' by Andrew Mckie, Ian Skeate, Gareth McAloon

'An Introduction to Beauty Negligence Claims – A Practical Guide for the Personal Injury Practitioner' by Greg Almond

'Intercompany Agreements for Transfer Pricing Compliance' by Paul Sutton

'Zen and the Art of Mediation' by Martin Plowman

'A Practical Guide to Adoption for Family Lawyers' by Graham Pegg

www.ingramcontent.com/pod-product-compliance
Lightning Source LLC
LaVergne TN
LVHW022114200926
848481LV00003B/1170
9781918241181